In Praise of My Husband Is Gay

"As a past facilitator of Straight Spouse Network and having professional experience with women at risk, I believe Carol is throwing out a lifeline to spouses in a sea of confusion and self doubt. Her manual gives women tools to navigate a difficult relationship shift. Carol's intimate story is absorbing."

MARY EVITTS, Former Women's Health Advocate
Boulder County Health Department

"At last! A book to hand to anyone dealing with having a gay spouse that will give them hope that they are not alone and that they can do more than survive! Out of the crucible of pain, in what many of us with gay family members experience as 'the unexpected journey,' Carol Grever has created a survival kit for straight spouses that offers hope and an opportunity for enormous personal growth. *My Husband is Gay* is a moving testament to the human capacity to endure what initially seems like a family tragedy and to make rich personal discoveries about resiliency in the process.

"I was genuinely moved by the weaving together of personal stories as a means of revealing the diverse ways each woman went through the process. I loved the book because it also gave me hope for relieving the pain I see in the straight spouses who come to PFLAG searching for understanding hearts and a road map to complete their journey."

JEAN HODGES, President
PFLAG Boulder, Colorado Chapter

"Carol's willingness to face her darkest fears and choose the path of love for herself and her ex-husband provides inspiration to all of us. This guidebook is a thoughtful map of the lives of may women and an essential resource for anyone facing the difficult terrain Carol has now charted with wisdom, common sense and an open heart."

DEBORAH BOWMAN, PH.D., Clinical Psychologist
Chair of Transpersonal Counseling Psychology
Naropa University, Boulder, Colorado

"I am impressed with Carol Grever's ability to pack so much substance and good reading into such a sensitive subject. Discovering your spouse is gay has to be one of life's most shocking moments. Carol not only tells her own personal story about that discovery, but also tells how she and other straight spouses dealt with the pain and struggled to find their way back to normalcy and happiness."

BARRIE HARMAN, Editor
Boulder, Colorado

my husband is gay

A Woman's Guide to Surviving the Crisis

Carol Grever

THE CROSSING PRESS
Berkeley | Toronto

The Crossing Press
A division of Ten Speed Press
P.O. Box 7123
Berkeley, California 94707
www.tenspeed.com

Distributed in Australia by Simon and Schuster Australia, in Canada by Ten Speed Press Canada, in New Zealand by Southern Publishers Group, in South Africa by Real Books, and in the United Kingdom and Europe by Airlift Book Company.

Library of Congress Cataloging-in-Publication Data on file with publisher.

Cover design by Petra Serafim
Interior design by Courtnay Perry
Cover photograph © Tamara Reynolds / Stone
Author photograph by Pamela J. Mayhew

First printing, 2001
Printed in the U.S.A.

2 3 4 5 6 7 8 9 10—09 08 07 06 05 04

Dedicated to my family, who steadfastly stand by, and to Dale, who walks beside me now.

I would like to acknowledge all the women who shared their stories with me and graciously allowed me to write about their experiences. They gave generously of their time and wisdom, often reliving very painful memories in the process. In every case, they did so because they were eager to help others. Their selfless courage was my inspiration.

Contents

Foreword

"Powerful! Poignant!" I exclaimed, putting down *My Husband is Gay*. This book echoes the voices of the 4,300 wives and husbands who have contacted me over the past fourteen years, weeping or incoherent as they tell me their spouses have come out as gay, lesbian, or bisexual. The women presented in these pages bring to life the struggle of spouses who get through the coming out crisis in one piece.

When my former husband came out in 1983, no book on the impact of disclosure on heterosexual spouses existed. Since then, a half a dozen have appeared, including my own about wives and husbands of homosexual or bisexual partners. Carol's book adds a quality work that weaves together her own experience with that of other wives. Her organization of the stories as stepping stones to survival—or beyond—brings straight spouses further into the public spotlight. Isolated, ignored, and invisible, they have remained hidden far too long in the closet their spouses left.

Coming out in marriage, first noted in the eighties, is a growing phenomenon affecting as many as two million couples in this country. Large numbers of the gay, lesbian, or bisexual spouses in these marriages have already disclosed their same-sex attractions or activities. More will do so later. Some never will. Disclosure devastates the straight spouses. Once spouses come out, the majority of marriages end, some quickly, others in time. A minority of couples stays together for three or more years.

A married person's coming out is not an individual event, but a family matter. His or her spouses and children, too, go through coming-out processes. All family members deal with the new identity of the spouse/parent, from different perspectives and at different age levels. The social context of the family adds another layer of pressures, since people hold diverse attitudes towards homosexuality. Community views about spouses who turn out to be gay or couples who remain married after disclosure, combined with concerns about "family values," fidelity, or divorce, can be extreme. The same brush that stereotypes the gay spouse stigmatizes the straight spouse as well, with comments like "Something must be wrong with you for marrying a gay person" or "Oh-oh. You must be an AIDS carrier." Often, it is easier to ignore a straight spouse's predicament.

In addition, few professionals have experience working with clients in this situation, especially straight spouses. The spouses' struggle to resolve disclosure concerns therefore becomes theirs alone. Such isolation intensifies their sense of being worthless, powerless, and hopeless. Feelings of sexual rejection increase as their partners' coming out is celebrated by gay or gay-positive organizations.

The basic challenge is: What does it mean that one of us is heterosexual and the other homosexual or bisexual? To answer, old ways of thinking need to be changed. This is a daunting task, since we in the Western World tend to think in either/or terms, dividing the world into two easy-to-manage packages: men/women, black/white, liberal/conservative, gay/straight. Within this dualistic paradigm, it is hard to comprehend how someone can be both gay and married. If a person marries, he or she must be heterosexual, especially if children are produced. Furthermore, such thinking goes, a person is either gay or straight. And, there is no such thing as bisexuality.

The experience of mixed-orientation couples proves otherwise. Their lives are painted in both/and terms and many shades of gay. As couples try to understand those complexities, they join the first ranks of researchers currently unveiling the real world of human sexuality. They are living the discovery, as the one spouse's disclosure destroys traditional concepts of sexuality and poses challenging dilemmas for both.

Faced by the spouse who discloses, the first dilemma is: How can I be honest with myself and not hurt my wife or husband—or be thrown out? Once he or she comes out, the straight spouse's puzzle is: How can my spouse be turned on by someone of the same gender rather than by me, whom he or she claims to love? Or, for someone with a bisexual spouse: How can he or she be attracted to me and also to someone else of the same gender? Both spouses wonder if it is possible to incorporate the new information into their marriage.

For wives whose husbands had secret liaisons before coming out, the disclosure presents a life-or-death question. They get tested for STDs and AIDS and wait anxiously for the results. These women cannot understand why their husbands, who profess to love them, put them at risk for a fatal disease or widowhood, not to mention the possibility that their children might become orphans.

In dealing with such issues, straight spouses report common issues and reactions, but each spouse forges an individual route—as the stories in this book illustrate. There is no single or "right" way to resolve these problems. Much depends on the spouse's resilience, the couple's relationship, and the support or lack thereof from their family and social, work, or religious associates.

Given the unexpected shattering of their trust and the lives they thought they had, small wonder that straight spouses feel devastated. As their shock wears off, emotions can be overwhelming. The pain is often so deep it is denied for months or years. Untreated, the hurt may become permanent, leading to a debilitating self-image as "victim." Anger runs through their coping: rage at the deception, at the way their husbands or wives came out to them, and at the fact that their mates are no longer straight. Outrage, however warranted, affects spouses' perceptions of what actually happened as well as their physical health. Untreated, it can lead to violence or self-destructive behavior. Finally, grief arises from their awareness of the loss of all they had, including their belief system and, in most cases, an intact family. Untreated, grief often leads to despair or suicidal behavior.

The energy of these negative feelings can be turned around to fuel spouses' actions in a positive direction. The key seems to be the ability to face and accept the reality of their situation and to redirect the unleashed forces toward working out a constructive outcome. Reality includes the disclosed orientation of their spouses and their own anguish. Unless these facts are acknowledged, healing and growth cannot begin.

Once spouses accept their partners' homosexuality or bisexuality, they can reconstruct their lives and their relationships with their partners, whether or not they stay married. No longer preoccupied with hurt and rage, they regain strength and achieve understanding. Accepting their losses as irretrievable, they nurture the most valuable things that remain and cultivate freshly discovered potential.

Part of this transformation occurs as spouses gain perspective on their suffering and see it as a human experience, not a gay-versus-straight issue. The shift comes with time but arrives more quickly if they find others who are coping with coming out problems. With peer support, many spouses gradually realize that no one is dealt a perfect set of cards; it is how one deals with a bad hand that makes the difference between real winning or losing.

Moving beyond the coming-out crisis—typically about three years—has allowed some spouses to forgive their partners, themselves, and anything else that may have contributed to the trauma. By letting go of vindictiveness, they found peace of mind. This doesn't mean they became doormats for abuse or forgot the hard lessons learned. Rather, they gained more clarity to focus on the last stages of their rocky path.

A number of spouses, after resolving their issues, help other spouses. Others educate the public about these issues and the idea that social change inevitably hurts someone. In the case of gay liberation, the disaster that befalls straight spouses needs to be considered, too. Still other spouses work toward widening society's acceptance of homosexuality so that persons who find they are not heterosexual will not feel they have to get married, leading to anguish for themselves, the women and men they marry, and the children they bring into the world.

Through such efforts, support for spouses has increased through the Straight Spouse Network (see Appendix), and media coverage has multiplied, from the *New York Times* and "20/20" to local newspapers, radio, and television. Yet, spouses without computers, those in the hinterlands, and others in conservative pockets of the country do not have access to or knowledge of support resources. Similarly, the growing publicity has not been enough to make concerns of straight spouses part of the public dialogue about justice for gay persons, anti-gay incidents, safe schools, or welcoming faith communities.

Heterosexual wives and husbands of gay, lesbian, or bisexual spouses need to be part of the public discussion about gay issues. They are an integral part of each other's lives. Since most mixed-orientation couples have children, the spouses remain linked as co-parents, even if they divorce. Whatever hurts the gay spouses hurts the straight spouses and their children.

Ignoring straight spouses slows their healing and makes it harder for them to resume productive lives. Discounting their plight shifts attention away from the core issue: Why do gay, lesbian, or bisexual people marry in the first place? The main factors for marrying, besides love and friendship, appear to include guilt, fear of rejection, and, often, an honest desire for marriage and children in pursuit of the American dream. To realize that dream, many suppress their same-sex attractions. Despite increasing public acceptance of homosexuality, fears still linger that they will be rejected by their families, employers, or faith communities if they disclose their sexual orientation. Thus, many continue to marry and, when their true feelings can no longer be repressed or their deception is discovered, innocent wives and husbands and their children are hurt.

The number of women and men contacting the Straight Spouse Network with such tales has doubled over the past year. These spouses, aged from twenty-something to over seventy, will value *My Husband is Gay* as peer support as well as guidance. Readers who are not spouses will find the book useful to understand an unforeseen consequence of gay liberation—the trauma that results when married men and women unexpectedly declare a different sexual orientation.

The problem needs to be addressed now, before more spouses are injured and families fractured. It is time for critics of gay people to ask whether their denigration of homosexuality really reinforces the family values they espouse, or whether they are in fact encouraging marriages that will most likely break up. It is time also for gay, lesbian, and bisexual persons considering marriage to ask themselves if they really want to harm the women and men they love and their unborn children, as well as themselves, by hiding or suppressing their true sexuality. They might ask themselves: Is that the justice we demand for ourselves? Is that the integrity we seek? For those who are already married and closeted, the questions are: What will be the cost of my dishonesty or risky behavior? Who may have to pay? What might be the reward of telling the truth?

Amity Pierce Buxton, Ph.D.
Author, *The Other Side of the Closet: The Coming-Out Crisis for Straight Spouses and Families*
Director, Straight Spouse Network
San Francisco, California
October, 2000

Introduction

"My husband is gay." When a heterosexual woman makes this statement, she is entering a strange land peopled by a secret sisterhood. Her initiation comes when she discovers that the man she married has a different sexual orientation from hers. Her dues may unknowingly have been paid over a long period of years, but the cost of membership in this private sorority escalates greatly from the moment she learns the truth about her own marriage.

Research indicates that more than two million homosexual or bisexual people are or have been married to heterosexual partners. While it is possible for these marriages to survive after the gay partner comes out, most end in divorce. Approximately 85 percent of these mixed-orientation couples eventually do separate, while the remaining 15 percent continue their marriage, usually with some mutually devised alternative contract.

My own marriage was one of those two million and one of the 85 percent. My husband and I had been married for more than thirty years when he told me that he "had homosexual tendencies," as he delicately understated it. That single moment changed both our lives forever, for once we know the truth, we cannot ever go back to ignorance.

Plunged into a totally unexpected crisis, I needed help but didn't know where to begin. I wanted practical information, guides, role models—some genuine resources for this frightening new journey. While volumes have been written to encourage homosexuals trying to come out, less information is available for the other half of each equation—the straight spouse whose life plan is irretrievably changed. Now, eight years later, after struggling through many stages toward recovery from my shock, I have written the book I needed to read then.

I began with my own journals. Four times I started to write this book; the first three times, I gave up in discouragement. Who would care to read about my private life? Later, I realized that my earlier attempts were self-centered and myopic. Here was a much more important opportunity—a chance to offer others the help I desperately needed but couldn't find during my earlier confusion. I also understood that the audience for this book needed more than one story to work with. They needed to hear the voices of many other women who had walked this path. I had to delve honestly into the experiences of other straight spouses, without sterilizing or generalizing—just telling their truths. With this broader, more altruistic motivation, the project moved from conceptual to situational, growing beyond my single experience to encompass the hard-earned lessons of many others.

I searched out dozens of other heterosexual wives of homosexual husbands, using advertising, networking, support group contacts, and referrals from health care professionals and related non-profits. The women I chose to interview varied in age, education, ethnicity, and socioeconomic status. Their homes are scattered between southern California and Vermont. In every case, they were enthusiastic about the project and eager to help other women in this situation. Patiently, they filled out detailed questionnaires, then spent hours talking with me, allowing me to record our interviews.

As I talked with more and more women, it became apparent that each person's experience was unique in its particulars, yet there were many common threads. Frequently, quotes in this book were spoken nearly word for word by more than one person, providing living illustration of recognizable steps from initial shock to eventual resolution. This progression from discovery to recovery is documented in a body of research on these issues. Therefore, each chapter describes a different stage of the progression, related to me in the interviews and recorded in the journals of my own experience.

This is not a scientific or clinical treatise of gay-straight marriages. Other authors, more objectively qualified as researchers and technical experts, have written those studies. Rather, this is a personal book, a survival manual offered from the point of view of the straight wife, sharing my story and that of other women who have suffered through similar challenges. It is about real people who found themselves imprisoned in a secret closet. It is about what we did to cope and what we learned.

Considered together, the women's accounts reinforce my hopeful thesis. Their courageous lives demonstrate that the discovery that one's husband is homosexual doesn't necessarily destroy the possibility of future happiness for either partner. Instead, this dramatic crisis may trigger a process of self-discovery and personal growth, leading to a higher level of honesty, insight, and inner strength. Though the women's names have been changed to protect their identity, their stories are recorded here as they were related to me. Without their generosity and candid conversation, this book could never have been written. I'm indebted to each of them.

So this is our book, carved out of the broken pieces of our unusual marriages. It tells of shock, suffering, confusion, betrayal, anger, illness, and despair. It tells of pain that was palpable and seemed endless, of secrecy and loneliness, isolation and disillusion. But recovery was the reward for those who courageously struggled through their pain. These women demonstrate the will to survive intact. No, to be even better! Their passage to wholeness exemplifies forgiveness, growth, healing, hope, and sometimes reconciliation. Their personal success is a triumph of newfound strength. In sharing our stories, we learned from each other. In offering others the wisdom of our experience, we affirm the possibility of new life beyond this crisis.

1

The Perfect Couple

Appearances may not reflect reality, particularly when it is necessary to hide a secret. If we could see into the thoughts of any of our friends, we'd be shocked at how little we really know of their lives. When a gay man marries a heterosexual woman, whether she is aware of his orientation or not, their outward appearance as a couple may be especially deceptive. Though they often seem like perfect couples, a different picture lies just beneath the surface.

How does this happen? Why do some gay men seek out straight spouses? Why do they marry at all? And why don't their wives suspect? How can these women be so blind—many times for decades? My husband and I were one of those "perfect couples." Our story may offer some clues.

Just One Example

When I was fifteen years old, I wrote in my diary that I wanted to marry Jim. Of course, he didn't know it! But I fell in love with him long before he noticed me at all. Then and later, I always knew that I loved him more than he loved me.

We met at our church's youth group when I was in the ninth grade and he was a high school sophomore. He attracted me immediately because he seemed so pure and upstanding. He didn't drink or smoke or swear, he was funny and fun and a leader of the group. I loved his soft Texas drawl, his intelligent blue eyes, and his beautiful smile. Since we attended schools in two adjacent towns, we only saw each other at church, which suddenly became the center of my innocent social world.

The Christian Youth Fellowship was an active one. My church friends and I sang in the choir together and did everything as a group, using Wednesday choir practice and Sunday night CYF meetings as our gathering place, then doing "fun stuff" afterward. The late 50s were an idyllic time, imbued with the family idealism of popular television shows like *Leave It to Beaver* and *Father Knows Best*. Jim was my teen ideal and remained my central romantic focus for decades afterward.

When Jim went to college, a year before I graduated from high school, I was completely loyal to him. We had dated through high school and I was utterly in love with him. The summer after I graduated from high school, he gave me his fraternity pin. I never had any other serious boyfriend. The next year, I followed Jim to college. It was a church-related liberal arts school, where our sheltered upbringing was completely supported by the campus environment. The expectation in our circles was to graduate from college with a "useful" degree (mine in teaching, his in business and religion), marry, have two children (no more), and serve society through hard work and a socially responsible profession. We and all our friends bought the whole package. I took advanced placement exams and gained extra credits in three sessions of summer school in order to catch up with Jim's class so we could graduate in the same year.

In our junior year Jim gave me an engagement ring, a sweet solitaire, set with his grandmother's diamond. All I wanted was to marry him! And that's what I did—over a semester break of that last year of college. I was twenty; Jim was twenty-one. We were both virgins. We were terribly young, terribly sheltered, terribly idealistic.

During our first year of marriage, we followed our families' traditional patterns. Living in graduate student housing, we were poor, but mostly happy. On our first wedding anniversary, my doctor confirmed that I was pregnant. Our second son was born twenty-seven months after the first. During that time frame, we lived in five different cities, pursuing summer jobs between graduate school terms and working to support our growing family. We landed in Portland where Jim had his first professional position as business administrator of the largest Christian church in Oregon. Money was still tight, but with my parents' help, I pursued my dream by studying for my master's degree in English. College teaching was my goal.

Like all young families, we did a balancing act; we were so busy in those years, they blur together. The Portland years were a time of huge growth and change for us both, though at first my childlike idealism remained intact. We appeared to be the perfect young couple, but slowly I began to have gnawing doubts and fears. Something important was missing. I became increasingly depressed, gained twenty pounds, and most days felt overwhelmed and lonely. My depression climaxed one rainy afternoon as I sat on my kitchen floor holding a butcher knife against my belly, thinking it would be easier to die. My baby's cry shook me back into the reality that someone really needed me—and I needed to be there for him. My sense of maternal responsibility saved my life that day.

My suicidal thoughts sent me into therapy, but after weeks of working with a counselor I couldn't relate to, nothing was resolved. So I ran. I decided to take our baby, Stephen, and go home to my parents in Tulsa, using the excuse of attending summer school there. I couldn't admit, even to myself, that this was a trial separation from Jim, but I knew that time and distance were essential for my survival. I longed for the sweet security of my parents' protection.

The summer in Tulsa was educational in many ways. First, I learned that I couldn't be happy in my childish cocoon. Indeed, one can never go back and relive a remembered situation. The shelter of my childhood felt repressive in my young adulthood. After six weeks, I knew that I had to face whatever was waiting in Portland. Stephen and I went back home. A few months afterward, I became pregnant for the second time. With two babies in the picture now, I knew that I had to make the marriage work, and we welcomed Gary into the world the following January.

What I didn't know was that Jim had begun acting on his "homosexual tendencies" about this time. Because of his fundamentalist upbringing, his experiments prompted deep guilt feelings. But his actions also taught him the best survival technique for all the years to follow: he learned to compartmentalize actions and feelings. He became an expert at leading two separate lives, one as a husband, father, and church professional, the other as an anonymous gay man. His two identities could be carefully stored in their respective compartments and skillfully retrieved as circumstances dictated. I'm convinced that this ability to put a lid on his other self saved his sanity. When his homosexual actions were put away, out of sight in his mental box, he actually could forget them and avoid the old guilt that had been instilled in him since the cradle. This was his key to survival.

The spring I graduated from Pacific University with my master's degree and a year's experience as a Teaching Assistant, Jim unexpectedly received an offer to accept an administrative position at Phillips University, our alma mater in Oklahoma. Coincidentally the school also had a temporary assignment open in the English department to replace a professor who was ill. I was ecstatic to land the job and we moved back to our roots.

Both of us felt that we had taken jobs that were too big for us, but we jumped into our challenging responsibilities with huge enthusiasm. I loved college teaching, and felt fully challenged and productive. I lost my excess weight, gained confidence, and felt I'd found my niche. The boys were changing from babies into healthy, noisy schoolboys. I juggled motherhood and professionalism through long evenings of class preparation and incredibly rewarding days.

Jim and I allowed our work to absorb us, though we also had a busy social life with close friends on the faculty. I felt more successful and confident than ever before. Students responded well in my classes and my teaching contract was renewed year after year. I also worked toward my doctorate. I finally had a real identity and sense of self outside of my marriage, and it felt wonderful to gain this new measure of independence.

Significantly, Jim traveled a lot in his student recruitment and alumni relations work. But it was a surprise the first time he decided to take a pleasure trip alone. Before that, our leisure travel had always been together. We had bought a used MG convertible that summer and he wanted to drive it by himself to California. He was gone for three weeks. This was the first of many such solo vacations. Now I understand why he liked to travel alone, but I had no inkling in those days.

During nearly seven years at the university, our life together degenerated. We disagreed on many key issues, particularly on administration/faculty conflicts. We lived in the same house, but we were drifting in different directions. I felt unsupported by Jim and increasingly frustrated by our lack of closeness. I flirted with our friends and flirted with disaster. It was apparent that our marriage was in serious trouble.

The situation reached a crisis when I confessed to Jim that I had fallen into an affair with one of our best friends. I was ripe for the attention and this man had given me the nurture and physical affection that I lacked at home—he made me feel beautiful and desirable and loved. But the guilt I carried became intolerable and I told Jim the whole story. Jim's response was that I could leave him, but if I did, he would never let the boys go with me. He used them as an effective lever. My kids needed both parents. I couldn't turn my back on that responsibility. I decided to break off the affair and stay with Jim. From that moment, he had the upper hand in our relationship: I was the guilty underdog. So much for self-esteem!

Expecting blame and condemnation from Jim as the days passed, I was surprised at his level of tolerance. He worked with me to pull the family back together as we received both joint and separate counseling with the minister of our church. After several intense months, it seemed best to move to a new place for a fresh start. What I didn't know was that our minister knew all along that Jim was gay, but urged him not to tell me. Whether it was to protect my husband or me, he successfully encouraged Jim to hide his true nature and to continue living the lie.

That spring, we shopped for a new life. During spring break, we drove north up the Front Range of the Rockies, from Albuquerque to northern Colorado, considering each town as a possible new home. Our requirements were that it be in or near the mountains and have a university nearby for cultural and educational breadth—and for possible employment opportunities. But employment was a big problem. We soon learned that a teacher and educational administrator were not in great demand at that time.

When we reached Boulder, Jim doggedly took his resumé into yet another private employment agency, where the owner shook his head and said he knew of no possible jobs for either of us. As he was leaving, almost as an afterthought, Jim inquired about any small businesses in town that might be for sale. The agency owner replied, "This one is."

That led us to a whole new possibility. We chatted about it all the way back to Oklahoma, fueling our enthusiasm and hope. If we went into business together, we could share goals, frustrations, wins, and losses. We would work as a team and perhaps heal the wounds in our marriage. We could finance the business initially by selling our Oklahoma house. Excitedly, we investigated this new idea of running a personnel service. The work would take advantage of Jim's business training and my communication skills. We thought that this joint enterprise would surely draw us closer together. That summer, we bought the nearly bankrupt employment agency and moved to Boulder on Labor Day.

For the next twenty-three years, we worked side by side, effective as equal partners in our successful entrepreneurial company.

After the first couple of years of sheer drudgery and financial uncertainty, we learned our new profession and began to feel more secure. Using our complementary skills, we grew the business from a Mom and Pop employment agency to a highly respected, multi-million dollar, diversified staffing company with multiple offices. Jim excelled in systems and accounting/finance, and I did well in marketing and communications. Numbers were his; words were mine. We became a superb professional team.

We were the envy of our friends. Everyone thought we had it all—Business success, wealth, community recognition, world travel, expensive "toys," and a glittering social life. That outer appearance mocked my growing knowledge that something very important was still missing. Privately, "the perfect couple" was hardly a couple at all. Our interests and activities and values were increasingly disparate. Private antagonisms were frequent. Each of us felt alone together in our house. The stress increased when Jim's father died after half a dozen years with Alzheimer's and my dad was diagnosed with leukemia.

I made many trips to Tulsa to be with my parents, saddened to watch the deterioration of my dad's health. I felt alienated from Jim, who seemed to carry on his nearly separate existence as if nothing were happening. My tension peaked when I spent nearly a whole month in Tulsa, sitting in Daddy's hospital room, watching his patient, brave battle with death. My sadness and grief were unspeakable. I was astounded at Jim's insensitivity to my needs when he chose to carry out his plans and travel alone to Hawaii for a convention and vacation. It was a trip we had planned and looked forward to together. Sitting in that hospital room in Tulsa, I felt utterly abandoned. There had been a lot of loneliness in my marriage, but this was too much.

Within the next few months, my sense of isolation grew. That spring, I tentatively suggested a trial separation. We had been married more than thirty years by then. Maybe I expected him to argue or disagree; maybe I wanted him to say, "Please, honey, let's fix what's wrong between us." Instead, he said he'd look for another place to live.

Friday afternoon before Memorial Day, Jim left to sign the lease on a house. As I often did, I retreated to my garden. Pruning and weeding were good therapy for a heart that was breaking. An hour later, Jim walked through the garden gate, looking terribly distraught. He slumped down on the retaining wall where I was working. I put down my pruning shears and sat beside him, facing the dying light over the mountains. For a long time neither of us spoke. Then, with a look of genuine anguish, his face pale and twisted, he said, "I don't want to leave…but I have to." Surprised by his obvious misery, I gently asked him to tell me more. Haltingly, he described his love for our home and his sense of utter loss in giving up the life we'd built so carefully. Finally, in a burst of pain, he told me his last awful secret, the one he'd carried all his life. "I have 'homosexual tendencies.'" Crystal clarity! In that one moment, everything in my life changed.

Jim's decision to tell me the whole truth was spontaneous, triggered by the imminent reality of his move. He hadn't planned to tell me because he was certain I'd reject him. He later said that it was as if someone else were speaking through him. After the first searing moment, we both realized that I did not reject him. I was not even angry…only shocked. Amazed by my deep calmness, I felt enormous sorrow for the exquisite pain he was in and the terrible cost of his thirty-year secret. Then for the first time in all our years together, Jim wept. He cried piteous tears, pent up his whole adult life. Watching his slumped body convulse with sobs, I felt genuine compassion for this husband whom I never really knew before. I held him in my arms for a long time, rocking him there on the garden wall.

It wasn't till later that I also felt stupid! It honestly had never, ever occurred to me that Jim had any secrets, much less that he lived a lie each day of his adult life! How could I have missed this fundamental fact? If I had been on an emotional roller coaster before, now I was in for the ride of my life. For the next few days, we processed information and emotions constantly, vacillating between despair and hope. I thought that I could accommodate his homosexuality, as long as he promised to stop lying to me. Total honesty was required. But as days passed, when he told me the naked truth about his past and present life, it hurt me to the core. Worst of all, I had to keep everything secret. It put me into the closet with Jim, in a lonely isolation beyond imagination.

Things got worse in mid-summer. My dad died on July 8. It helped that both my mother and I were with him, holding each of his hands and giving him gentle permission to let go of his valiant struggle. He died peacefully with the same dignity he'd carried through life and through his final, awful illness. I was devastated. My grief was a black, bottomless hole. Within one year, I had lost the three men I'd loved most in my life—my father, Jim's father, and Jim himself. All the tears I'd dammed behind a strong will gushed through this valley of loss. I cried and cried, thinking I'd never stop.

Back in Boulder, Jim and I struggled in our effort to stay together. Our arrangement was that either of us could go out with other men, with the agreement that we would not keep any secrets. Jim enjoyed a widening circle of gay friends. After an evening out, he'd come back flushed with excitement and eager to talk about his experiences. I stayed at home. Though I had "permission" to pursue pleasure with others, I lacked the energy and nerve. I was terrified by the prospect. So I worked days and stayed home alone at night.

As months passed, I became resentful that Jim enjoyed everything he wanted and I did not. I languished while he relished his double life ever more actively, his secret sexual orientation cloaked by our long-term marriage. The inequity of the whole situation wounded me terribly. I felt lonely and cheated. Worse, I felt utterly inauthentic, pretending to the outer world that our marriage was ideal, knowing that it wasn't even a marriage. Lies and half-truths were a daily necessity. I couldn't even talk honestly with my own mother. There was no security anywhere. My greatest fear had always been to be alone, and now that seemed inevitable.

Jim was also suffering. Though the cover of our marriage protected him from society's judgment, he was not free to express himself fully as a gay man. His ambivalence was becoming more painful by the day, and his gay support groups urged him to make the break. But he also feared a lonely future. Our long-term relationship had made us co-dependent. With this heavy uncertainty, we staggered through many months.

We were both in therapy, but I became frightened by my wild mood swings. Sometimes I felt absolutely crazy. Clearly, only I could heal myself and I had to find the way. Years before, I had left the conservative church of my childhood and now desperately needed spiritual support. I tried meditation, hoping for relief. It helped more than anything, so I enrolled in a Shambhala Training weekend to learn more about it. Sitting meditation, based on Tibetan Buddhist practice, gave me an encouraging glimpse of peace previously unknown.

But as Jim grew more distant and I felt more isolated, the day came when I looked in the mirror and said, "What's in this for me? What about me!" I finally knew. I couldn't spend the rest of my days accommodating someone else's needs at the expense of my own. I had to create a new life for myself. I had to face my fear of loneliness and end our marriage. That moment of insight freed me.

It took a long time! Our careers, our business, our investments, our home, our office building, all our possessions had been jointly earned and were jointly held. We had spent more than thirty years building a life that now had to be dismantled. I grieved that like a death. One unexpected advantage of the slow, complicated separation, however, was that it gave us time to process all the change in a more subtle way. It taught us a new measure of patience to extricate ourselves, especially since we were both determined not to attack and harm each other further. Still, the stress was wrenching. We were uprooting everything! Finally, we accomplished the sale of our business. After some surprises and one major confrontation about fair shares, we completed the division of assets and property.

Meanwhile I had participated in thirteen weekend meditation programs over two years at the Shambhala Center. I was comforted by this practice that helped me feel my raw, tender, bruised, vulnerable heart in a new way. The spiritual underpinnings of meditation practice allowed me to work with my personal situation as it unfolded, day after day, with the courage of a gentle warrior. It trained me to stay present in the moment, not agonizing over past or future. It emphasized the Basic Goodness and interconnectedness of all sentient beings. I began to realize that Jim and I were not so different in our pain and that it was an act of love to let him go. He needed authenticity as much as I did. The long process of selling the business actually became an advantage—It gave me time to prepare spiritually for our separation. On July 2, 1994, I took action on what I'd known in my heart for many months. I took refuge in the Buddha, the Dharma, and the Sangha—the teacher, the teachings, and the spiritual community. I became a Buddhist.

Before he moved from our home, Jim decided to come out to all our family. I encouraged complete openness. I was suffocating in the closet of secrecy! Besides, without knowing the truth, how could they ever understand our separation? Typically, we went together to each relative. We told Jim's mother first, then traveled to Oklahoma and California to see my mother and our two sons. Jim was panic-stricken, but I stayed with him through the frightful meetings. Telling his mother was hardest, I think, especially when her response was, "I'd rather have heard that you were dying." But after her shock subsided, she gradually became more accepting. The others seemed less judgmental. I was so proud of our son Steve's summary: "Dad, there's nothing you could ever do that would make me stop loving you." Jim felt relieved and I felt free!

Jim bought a new house and moved the spring before the business sale was final. I stayed in our old home, comforted by its familiarity and my healing garden. A few months later I filed for divorce. It was significant that we had tediously settled our financial affairs before this, because it enabled us to use the same lawyer and to maintain civility through the divorce. We were determined to salvage as much friendship as we could, honoring our long history together and the preciousness of our remaining family ties. Our divorce attorney said it was the most amicable procedure he'd ever handled. Our divorce was final in April 1996, five years after Jim's disclosure to me of his homosexual orientation. Our marriage lasted thirty-five years.

Why Do Gays Marry?

The outline of personal experience you've just read shows the history of only one gay/straight marriage. There are many variations. Commonly accepted research indicates that two percent of all married men are basically homosexual. One out of every five gay men is married, or has been in the past. This implies that many of the men who take part in gay sexual encounters are married to wives who are unaware of their homosexual orientation and activities.

But why do these men marry heterosexual women in the first place? Such marriages usually fail and leave a trail of destruction as they disintegrate.

Denial and Lack of Awareness

The most basic reason is denial of their sexual orientation. Disturbed or frightened by their feelings, they may believe that marriage will help their same-sex desire disappear. They may want to change this aspect of themselves and believe that a sexual and marital commitment to a woman will achieve the difference.

Several clear examples of this reasoning emerged among the women I interviewed. One extreme case was Laura's. Only after her husband experienced heart trouble and became clinically depressed did he realize that "he could not go on being deceptive." Only then did he decide to disclose his sexual orientation. Now seventy years old and still married to her gay husband, she described his revelation twenty years earlier as bewildering. "He sat me down in a chair and sat on a footstool in front of me and told me that his mother was right when she told me that he was homosexual. At that time, homosexuality did not mean anything to me, other than he liked men. I knew nothing about the sexual part. Neither of our families ever talked about sex."

Though she had been given the same information twenty years before, she had managed to ignore it and forget it. Laura and her husband had both spent nearly forty years in denial!

This case also illustrates another common factor: lack of awareness. Because of their age and the Victorian mores of their youth, Laura and her husband were uninformed. Ignorance about sex in general was the norm as they grew up. Most American families simply didn't discuss such issues. Indeed, Laura had to look up the word *homosexual* in a medical dictionary before she began to understand the implications of her husband's disclosure. But, she said, "it still didn't click." She added, "even though he knew he was different at age six, he really did not know much about sexual orientation." So the two of them, having lived as a couple for decades, sought information together in a technical book recommended by his psychiatrist. It appears that Laura's husband married her hoping to deny or change his basic nature. He had to get physically and emotionally ill before he was forced to face his truth.

Kaye's story offers another example of both denial and a gay husband's attempt to change. In a letter attached to her questionnaire, she wrote, "My story is such a convoluted one because the real wrestle with the reality of Joseph's homosexuality didn't occur until almost fifteen years after he first told me about it."

Like Laura, Kaye has chosen to remain married, despite the fact that she has known of her husband's homosexuality for twenty-eight years.

For Kaye, there were two disclosures. The first occurred when her two children were around eight and twelve years old, probably in 1971 or '72. "He told me on a walk one evening. It seems like it came out of the blue. I don't remember a preamble. He just said he'd begun to realize he wasn't like some men when it came to sex—that he looked at it differently. My immediate reaction was to say that I knew and that it was no big deal. He said he didn't think I understood. I assured him I did. He said he was bisexual and I said I'd had that sense for many years. He explained that my cousin had been his first experience (and the only one at that point)."

She perceived Joseph's confession as an incident, acknowledging that he was bisexual, i.e., not really gay. Moreover, he wanted to remain married, to stay with her and their children. Because of their mutual love, she agreed to that and for years afterward chose not to notice indications of Joseph's gay activities. "There were subsequently several occasions on which I guessed he'd been with someone, but it was only a half-conscious guess that didn't reach the level of knowing."

Joseph's second disclosure to Kaye came later, in 1983, and was much more traumatic because it revealed "an established relationship and a history of occasional (perhaps even frequent) casual encounters." Joseph seemed poised for some major change. "I remember that during that time I had an unusual experience of fear. I became conscious of the fear when I began having trouble breathing. My chest was tight and I had to take deep breaths every few minutes to get enough air. My pulse would race and a feeling of imminent doom would wash over me. I decided Joseph was about to tell me he was leaving me. This was shortly after he began therapy and before he began to talk to me about his sexual orientation again."

Both Kaye and Joseph were still in denial, Kaye carefully protecting her own state of ignorance. She didn't want to know the whole truth. "My sense of impending doom lasted about a week and then, one night, amid a flood of his own tears, Joseph told me he needed to move out for a while because he needed the distance in order to sort things out. When I asked if he were considering divorce, he said he wasn't. I must say I was relieved, since I had been dreading his wanting to leave permanently. He was just saying he needed space for a while. Since I'd had fantasies many times over the years of taking a year off by myself just to catch my breath, I wasn't threatened by his deciding to do so."

There is much more to this interesting story, but suffice to say that this couple's determination to remain in their marriage has been supported, often at great cost, by both denial and lack of awareness. They have been married for thirty-eight years, though Kaye describes their relationship as "a roller coaster ride—ranging from despair to joy."

Though I didn't realize it at the time, I also used denial as a tool to keep my marriage intact, particularly before Jim came out to me. I knew something was wrong, but was afraid to know the truth. This journal entry illustrates. "Jim left this morning for another of his solo vacations. This time it's a scuba diving trip to the Bahamas. He's never been particularly athletic, but in the past few years has discovered that he's adept at water skiing and boating and now he's extending his water sports to reef diving.

"Though we started the scuba classes together, I dropped out before my deep-water tests because of increasing claustrophobia under water. It's clear to me anyway that Jim would rather do these trips alone.

"He plans to complete his tests for diving certification on this trip and is signed up with a dive shop tour that provides tanks, provisions, and a dive boat for a week. Like me, he's reaching out for something fresh and exciting, but even more, he's desperately fighting the changes of middle-age.

"Jim's new sport is just another example of the division growing between us. He really doesn't want to include me in most of his social activities. I feel him pulling away; his indifference is palpable. Though I always feel lonely, it's almost a relief for him to be physically out of town, since he has been emotionally absent anyway. I can relax for awhile, knowing there will be no demands for a few days.

"Jim's mother is terribly inquisitive about what's happening to us. Answering her loaded questions is getting harder, though I'm determined to be honest, as in the letter I wrote to her today: 'You ask if Jim is in a mid-life crisis. Of course!—though I'm not sure what that means or where it will lead. For months, he's been in a buying frenzy: bright, youthful clothes, expensive toys (thousands in diving equipment, for example), a vacation by himself in the Bahamas, an extravagant blue Mercedes Benz. He exercises obsessively in four or five aerobics classes a week, pursuing unnatural thinness. Most of his friends are single and younger. Last week, he dyed his graying eyebrows! Poor Jim is driving himself mercilessly in pursuit of youth and happiness. He's literally chasing it around the world. And he's doing it alone—or at least without me. My hope is that his journey will end where it began, here at home. I'll be waiting.'" Ignorance may not be bliss, but sometimes it feels safer to retreat to its protective cocoon.

In all three of these cases, the homosexual husbands became increasingly restless after many years of marriage, leading to their decision to come out in middle-age or even later. It is interesting to note that the age at which a married man comes to terms with his homosexuality may be influenced by his socio-economic status. Dr. Raj Persaud, a consultant psychiatrist at Maudsley Hospital in England, points out two main patterns, which depend on social class. Homosexual activity peaks during the late teens or early twenties for men with lower incomes and status, then declines thereafter. Dr. Persaud observes that poorer gays are most attractive to other homosexual men during their youth, so their opportunities for sexual encounters are greater then. In contrast, gay married men in the higher social strata increase their homosexual activities as they grow older. Upper class gays find that their opportunities grow with increasing income levels. Their wealth attracts younger men and they have the resources to arrange clandestine meetings. High-powered jobs also allow them to travel alone, away from their families. Thus, they indulge their homosexual desires later in life.

Dr. Persaud's observation helps explain both the early denial and growing restlessness evident in all of the mature men in the three cases cited. Jim's expensive trips and toys also fit the pattern. Further, it sheds light on the frequency of wide age differences in gay couples. One woman I interviewed was dismayed when she learned that her sixty-one-year-old husband was involved with a thirty-four-year-old man. She thought it was pitiful that her husband's lover was just a year older than his own son.

Social and Religious Expectations

A second major reason that gay men marry is to conform to family or career or societal expectations. In each of the three examples already given, the couples married because it was the social norm. It was the American "Ozzie and Harriet" pattern of the '40s and '50s.

Two women I spoke with—Laura and Vera—are now in their 70s. Both stayed married for decades after they learned of their husbands' homosexuality; both continued meeting societal expectations of "perfect couples." Vera, now 74, was a particularly interesting case. Her marriage to Hank seemed excellent for the first fourteen years. They had two children, a boy and a girl, and Vera said Hank was "very attentive and committed to me, our children, and their welfare."

Life changed when Hank got into trouble in the Air Force, after spending fourteen years achieving the rank of Captain. Their dreams and expectation of a long military career ended. He had become sexually involved with the associate pastor of their church, who was also married, but was either bisexual or gay. The episode led to Hank's general discharge from the Air Force and a complete change of careers for both him and Vera. "It was just a mistake," he promised Vera, convincing her to stay in their marriage. She agreed, but notes that their sexual contact soon ended altogether.

For nearly twenty years longer, they remained in what Vera described as a marriage of friendship. They stayed together, maintaining their public façade. Much later, Vera learned that through these years Hank continued his clandestine homosexual contacts. She wrote, "My husband was living a double life. He was lay-leader of church, with many other church volunteer jobs.

He was also the precinct committeeman for those conservative Republicans!"

But Hank's hidden life eventually caught up with him. He died with AIDS in 1985. Vera points out one of many ironies: "What a big, big funeral, with no knowledge (on the part of his conservative friends) of his real lifestyle."

Until I spoke with Vera, she never told this story to anyone except her children and her brother and sister. The children learned of their father's sexual orientation and the reason for his illness only a few weeks before his death. None of Vera's friends know to this day. Here is an example of a mature lady living up to her lifelong perception of society's expectations.

A sub-category of social expectation is religious pressure. For example, Rob's wife reported that he "is hung up on fundamentalist religion." Though he has known since the third grade that he is gay, his sexual orientation wasn't allowed by his Southern Baptist upbringing. He chose to marry and hide behind a strong wife. After an unsuccessful marriage and eventual divorce, Rob converted to Mormonism and went to a Mormon therapist to try to get over being gay. He was unsuccessful.

Fear of Economic Loss

Fear is the cornerstone of the third important reason that gay men marry. There is often great risk in being openly gay. The disguise of marriage offers a cover for homosexuals' true orientation and allows them to pass in the broader society. Besides aiding personal safety and providing social acceptance, marriage can also protect a man's career path, assuring upward mobility, particularly in more conservative professions.

Several of the women I interviewed were wives of professionals in highly paid, highly visible positions (psychiatrist, medical doctor, university administrator, military officer, public school superintendent, and business owner). All of these men were convinced that coming out publicly would be disastrous or at least detrimental to their careers. In fact, both the military officer and the school superintendent lost their jobs when their sexual orientation was discovered. For all these couples, the men's careers and the family's economic future were safer as long as they stayed married and in the closet. Wealthier, educated gays often marry because it is a choice that protects their livelihood.

At the other end of the economic scale, sheer necessity may influence a homosexual to marry because he needs a second income. Betty's story is the most extreme I found. She worked as a nurse for eleven years to pay for her husband's college education, deferring her own higher education until he got his degree. (He claimed at the outset that he could complete a degree program in two years, but Betty now knows "this was a time of great sexual fantasy and delight for him," so he didn't hurry to finish.) She never had the chance to go back to school, and now that they have ended their somewhat violent twenty-five-year marriage, she receives no child support or other financial help from her ex-husband. She is seriously ill and has been reduced to poverty, struggling to get by on a $10,000 annual income. I asked about her lowest point. She replied, "Facing a long-term terminal illness, no housing, no job, no food, no financial security, and no place to go, I had to approach the state social services department for assistance for the first time in my life."

Ill, destitute, and entirely responsible for her two young children, she depends on county welfare, food stamps, and subsidized housing. As this sad story illustrates, money has a definite influence on who marries and who stays married.

The reasons to marry discussed so far are all based on fear. Denial and lack of awareness relate to the fear of finding out and knowing the naked truth. Bowing to social or religious expectation is rooted in the fear of rejection. And career ambition is partly related to economic insecurity and fear of want. The last two major reasons gays marry are quite different from these.

Desire for Children or Companionship

I learned that some gay men marry because they desire progeny and the long-term companionship of a family that includes children. I spoke with several gay men who wanted to father a child and married partly for that reason. One man said that when he and his wife were trying to conceive, they would race up the stairs two or three at a time, in their hurry to have sex. "We couldn't wait, both children were so wanted."

A twist on this theme was evident in the case of Sandy and James. She was a straight wife who knew from the beginning about her husband's homosexuality, but made a conscious decision to have his child before she left him. Longing to have a baby, she had experienced great difficulty in getting pregnant through several previous years with James and was aware that her childbearing time was limited. She felt that because of her age she needed to have her baby first, then leave her husband. She consciously, carefully accomplished her plan through artificial insemination, then filed for divorce when her daughter was two years old.

In another instance, Rita is the caregiver for her bisexual husband who is confined to a wheelchair. They have been married for twenty-nine years. She learned of his sexual orientation in 1977. Though she described their marriage as stressful and not satisfying, particularly in the early years, they "stayed together by choice and intention." They apparently sublimate their needs through focusing on their altruistic careers. She describes herself as "an unusually loving person" who has overcome early sexual abuse through an advocacy role and a sense of vocation. Both are deeply religious and actively committed to helping others in the gay and lesbian community.

There are other familial needs that a wife fulfills for a gay husband, aside from caregiving or bearing children. Traditional wives, as seen in the examples earlier in the chapter, can be agreeable companions and social partners. Their presence supports a professional man's career ambition. And when he is off work, they help create a comfortable, attractive home—a refuge from career pressures. These wives may provide a needed second income or run an efficient, money-saving household.

And we must not ignore love! Sincere affection and abiding love are often expressed by many gay/straight couples, both before and after disclosure of the man's homosexuality. Obviously, homosexual and heterosexual men may marry for many of the same traditional reasons.

Adventure In Alternative Lifestyles

In contrast to traditional, old-fashioned matches, several of the women I interviewed married gay or bisexual men with full prior knowledge of their sexual differences. They tended to be younger people, activists or idealists, often with a confrontational bent.

Take, for example, Cherie and Roy. Though she is straight, she met Roy at a gay bar in 1991. "We have the same taste in pickups, music, and men!" she laughs. They first became good friends, having great, raucous times, then decided to live together in 1993. Later, they married, with an open contract and full disclosure of their extra-marital activities. Though they have experienced some difficulties and are in counseling together now, Cherie insists that "these marriages can work!" and feels that she is enriched by Roy's presence.

In another case, Annie knew before they were married that Jack was bisexual. "I thought that indicated how liberal we both were. I didn't see it as a threat. We were married in 1976 at a time when it seemed fashionable to have no rules. Let it happen! We admired each other, but now I know we knew too little to have a deep love commitment or plan about how to run a marriage. We actually got married because I was pregnant. Our sex life deteriorated from that point. Of course, I felt rejected and undesirable, but Jack backed away from sex with excuses like not wanting to harm the baby during my pregnancy. We never really had a sex life after that, other than enough to have one more child three years later."

Another interesting example of alternative lifestyle as a choice is seen in Zoe and Charles. Zoe is a former actress who worked in England and the United States before her marriage. She was very active sexually before her marriage and was always attracted to gay men, as well as straight. She converted to Buddhism many years ago and followed a Buddhist teacher who happened to be bisexual. After her teacher died of AIDS, she met and married her bisexual husband, Charles.

Buddhism teaches that all experiences are learning opportunities, "fuel for waking up." Zoe says her marriage taught her to be more compassionate with herself and others, keeping her from her old habits of self-deprecation and blame. She believes that Charles, also a long-time Buddhist, chose to marry her because he was defensive about his sexual orientation—"he hasn't really come to terms with it"—and the marriage is a cover. His parents are also still in denial. Though Zoe's marriage is definitely unusual, it seems to meet the needs of both partners, at least for the present. They have just adopted a daughter (she believes the child has helped the marriage) and they do give the outer appearance of a perfect couple.

So back to the central question: Why do gay men so often marry? There are many private reasons, of course, and only the most obvious ones have been cited. As one formerly married homosexual summarized, "Until attitudes change, I think people will continue getting married as I did, for the sake of respectability, to stop wagging tongues, to appease society, to please one's parents, and to make it as easy as possible to get on with life."

Why Do Gays Stay Married?

About fifteen percent of the gay men who marry stay in that relationship. Several motivations are immediately apparent. Gays may remain married because of fear or economic or career considerations. There is a reluctance to disrupt life as it is—to go through the pain of starting over. Some stay with their wives in order to protect family members from knowledge of their sexual orientation. Others stay married because of their attachment to their children and their fear of losing touch with them. A few, who are ill or disabled, may be forced to stay married because their wives are also their caregivers. And finally, religious conviction plays a strong role for some individuals.

The husbands and wives you've met in this chapter will surface again throughout the book, along with many others. As the threads of their stories cross, these living examples of straight spouse survival will weave a tapestry of recognition and courage.

2

Coming Out and
Its Fallout

When Jim sat on the garden wall with me and told me he had homosexual tendencies, he was in extreme emotional pain. He had been acting on those tendencies for a long time, of course, but had successfully compartmentalized his actions—out of sight, out of mind. He had also successfully deceived me for nearly thirty years. When I asked for a separation that spring, it forced the issue and he began to tell me the truth.

Why didn't I suspect? An entry from my journal shows some of the clues I saw earlier, but didn't comprehend. "All day cleaning winter's debris from the garden, I was thinking about Jim. Here's how it is with Jim and me. After more than thirty years of marriage (maybe twenty-five of which were reasonably happy), I feel really alone. We have less and less in common. Our continuing drive to sell the business is connected to our growing insecurity in our marriage. It would be unthinkable to work so closely together at the office if we ultimately live apart. After our business is gone, what will be left between us? Only history? Convenience? Pride? Is that enough to stay married?

"Jim communicates less and less and seeks companionship away from home. He has his friends; I have mine. His interests are increasingly different from mine and he is obsessed with youth. Flashy clothes and expensive toys excite him. I don't.

"As he pointed out to me during an argument this morning, we never had common interests. He likes movies, I like to read; he likes oldies, I like New Age music; he likes city excitement, I like quiet mountain walks. On and on. No one's to blame—we are who we are. Still, it is depressing for a married couple to work so hard at finding even a few activities we can share and both enjoy.

"As I increasingly look inward, it is less important to keep up the old front, make an impression, or spend time with people I don't care about. My circle of friends narrows but deepens by the year. I'm delegating as much of my responsibility in the business as possible, pulling away from public view, step by step. In contrast, Jim seems compelled to surround himself with crowds of jazzy kids. He dresses like a twenty year-old, following absurd fads. He dyes his hair and shaves off his graying beard. All of his energy is directed toward the surface. Andy Warhol nailed it: Jim is deeply superficial. I'm sick over our separation of spirit."

If I had even remotely suspected the reason for these changes in my formerly conventional mate, I would not have experienced such utter shock at Jim's disclosure. I was truly unaware. All I knew was that I felt unhappy and somehow abandoned. Fortunately for both of us Jim's genuine anguish touched me so deeply that I responded to his confession with compassion rather than anger. Those first crucial hours allowed us to feel closer again, at least while I adjusted to this new knowledge. We treated each other with concern, able to call on the love that remained.

Though I certainly didn't realize it at the time, I was one of the lucky ones.

A Critical Moment

How a wife learns of her husband's homosexuality helps determine the eventual outcome of their marriage and the nature of any future relationship with each other. The circumstances surrounding his disclosure also affect their immediate behavior and their later level of self-esteem. It is a critical moment. A happy ending is unlikely if this discovery occurs in a shocking or insensitive setting.

Betty, whom we met in the first chapter, offers one negative example. Though she and Rob were married for twenty-five years, theirs was an abusive relationship marked by verbal insults and physical explosions—a pattern repeated from Rob's own abused childhood. The day after their wedding night she angered him and he hit her so hard that he knocked her down. That was only the beginning. Years later, Rob's disclosure of his homosexuality was unexpected, quick, and nasty. It was unfortunately typical of their whole history. Betty recalls, "My husband came to me at 10:10 P.M., woke me, and stated he was gay and had been all along. He further stated he knew he was gay since third grade. He told me he had to hide behind a strong woman because he knew from his fundamentalist religious upbringing that this was not acceptable, so he chose to hide. He then left the house."

After her initial reaction of complete shock, Betty tried to deny this reality in her own mind, but soon felt "stupid and angry at having been deceived for so many years." She saw clearly for the first time that he had used her. While she worked as a nurse in a mountain community to support his college expenses, Rob had lived out his homosexual dreams in his city apartment. No wonder it took him eleven years to finish school! Rob moved away immediately after his disclosure, and Betty filed for the divorce that he requested.

Betty heard a blunt statement from Rob, but other cases showed that actions rather than words sometimes precipitate recognition of the husband's true orientation. Lydia's case is an example. This marriage, too, had been hard from the start. Jonathan was a public school music teacher and she was a stay-at-home mom with their three children. Lydia went to a neighboring state one year to visit her parents around Christmas while their pre-teen children stayed at home with their father. "As soon as I left town, Jonathan called a male friend in the city to come immediately to our town. One of the children reported to me they were in the bedroom all the time. I was torn apart totally at that invasion into the household. Jonathan saw nothing wrong with it. That January Jonathan found out this friend tested positive for HIV, so he needed to go to the city to be tested and wanted me to go also."

Jonathan's act was not completely surprising. Lydia had reasons to suspect Jonathan's sexual orientation ten years earlier. "There were some suspicions about his relationships with high school boys in the school where he taught. One boy was gay and spent a lot of time with Jonathan and even sent him flowers." Her husband often told her he had to work late at school, but several times when Lydia drove by the campus, his car wasn't there. He also corresponded with several men who lived out of state and occasionally received gifts from them. Lydia managed to ignore the implication of these incidents until Jonathan brazenly entertained a lover in their bedroom that fateful Christmas. His boldness forced her to recognize the truth.

As Lydia's story illustrates, many wives experience a growing awareness of their husband's orientation over a period of years, rather than facing the shock of a single, unexpected statement. Similarly, Kaye's husband told her somewhat obliquely during a quiet walk in the early 1970s. She brushed it aside at the time and ignored many clues of his further deception until he confessed more clearly in 1983. That second disclosure was more traumatic for Kaye because Joseph then moved out of their home to live with his male lover. In both of these cases, actions took place over many years that finally led each wife to face the full reality of her husband's homosexuality.

The outcome for each couple was quite different, however, because of the circumstances surrounding the direct disclosure. Betty's experience was harsh and cruel, while Kaye's was more gentle and civilized, evolving over a long time. Betty divorced her husband almost immediately. In contrast, Joseph moved back home after six months and he and Kaye are still married. Part of the difference in these outcomes relates to the way in which the women learned the truth.

Some Gentler Outings

Some wives have the benefit of a gentler landing when they get the bad news. Less trauma in the beginning implies a happier ending. The circumstances of disclosure seem largely dependent upon the couple's previous relationship through their years of marriage. Individual personalities and the level of their general stability obviously play huge roles in the drama.

Carlotta and Daniel were married for twenty-four years and "shared a very strong commitment to each other" and their family. They worked hard at their professions; both hold doctorates and are passionate about improving the quality of public school education. In fact, Carlotta described her school superintendent husband as a workaholic.

In June, 1992, Carlotta underwent a hysterectomy. As several months passed, she thought it odd that she and Daniel did not resume sexual relations. "The following October, on a weekend trip to the mountains, I asked if we were ever going to make love again. That's when he told me he thought he was gay. At first I laughed. I felt overwhelming relief that it wasn't me! Then we had a very caring talk about what our relationship had been like and what the future might look like for him. That night we confirmed that our marriage was over."

But Carlotta and Daniel continued to cooperate for many months afterward to create a course of action that would be least harmful to all concerned. They worked together to buy and furnish a new home for Carlotta, waited six months to tell their children what was happening, then separated very discreetly, shielding both their careers. They remained mutually supportive. Carlotta set up Daniel's new kitchen and helped him move into his nearby apartment, which he soon shared with his gay lover.

Through a four-year transition out of their long marriage, their mutual love and respect allowed them to move forward deliberately without intentionally hurting each other. Their children also had time to adjust to their new reality. Carlotta later said that she "worked very hard at Daniel's being successful at being gay." Their amicable divorce was final in 1996. They worked out the details of their settlement themselves, without a lawyer.

A Faster Track

Not all the gay husbands waited so long to come out. Lee and Randy met in junior high school and dated occasionally when she was away at college. She dated several other men, but always came back to him. "We had come from similar backgrounds, and our fathers had worked together for several years." When one of Lee's friends had a date with Randy, "she called me up to say that I needed to talk to Randy, as all they had talked about on their date was me." The match seemed right. Five months before her college graduation, Randy asked Lee to marry him. They set their wedding date shortly after her commencement. She recalls, "We went out with our group of friends for a big party the weekend before the wedding. On our way back, he said there was something that he should probably tell me, but just couldn't. I told him that if it was going to affect my life, that he probably should. But he didn't."

They married two weeks after Lee's graduation. It was a big, expensive wedding in the local Catholic Church. The reception was in the backyard of Lee's childhood home. She remembers, "I really thought that I was on my way to a perfect life with a wonderful guy."

But the honeymoon held a big surprise. "We flew to Portland, Oregon, and rented a car for our honeymoon. We drove up the Oregon coast to Seattle and stayed in nice hotels, including a wonderful place called Salishan Lodge. The setting was very romantic and relaxing. The first thing that struck me as odd was that he made a negative comment about the lingerie I had brought—a different nightie for every night. He didn't want to be close physically. Finally, on Thursday night, he admitted that he should have told me something before we got married. After a couple of hours of trying to drag it out of him, he finally said that he thought he was gay.

"It had never, ever crossed my mind. Gay men didn't marry women! They were into men! How was I supposed to handle this? He didn't say he was gay, and he didn't say he wasn't. And how was I going to go home and tell my family? So we decided to come home and get counseling—not to 'fix' him, but to see if this marriage could work under these circumstances."

Eloquent Actions

Sometimes covert actions rather than words expose a gay husband's secret. Andrea's marriage had never been ideal. She described it as difficult and dishonest, even before she discovered her husband's homosexuality. That discovery came when workmen removed a ceiling tile in the basement, revealing two boxes. The workers called her, and she found that the boxes contained homosexual videos, sex toys, paraphernalia, and transgender clothing. This is a good example of complete deception and utter surprise. Andrea's immediate reaction was hysteria, terror, and panic.

Bonnie's discovery was also accidental. She came upon a letter her husband had written to a mutual friend, describing the men's gay encounter. Bonnie said, "At the time, I didn't know our friend was gay. I didn't recognize anyone who was gay. I didn't even know the words homophobia, gay, or bisexual. I was a college graduate, but I felt very unlearned."

Bonnie found that revealing letter one weekday morning. Her spouse was an elementary teacher and was working at his school. "I somehow survived the day. I couldn't wait until he came home and we could talk. Our sons were in the backyard playing and my husband and I had a visit!"

Bonnie and Andrea had both been married for a number of years before their big surprise. Some women find out sooner. Joni was still in her mid-twenties when she discovered her husband's homosexuality after only two and a half years of marriage. She described those first years as great—loving, caring, and wonderful. "We were very happy and believed in each other 100%." David courted her in college and was her first love, a perfect prince charming, but she grew more concerned as time passed. She was worried when David started coming home later and later from his accounting office. Was he having an affair with another woman? Was there something wrong with her?

Her fears deepened when David began to bring home adult videos of bisexual and group sexual encounters, urging her to watch the movies with him. At first, she thought his fascination with the subject mere fantasy, but eventually he suggested that they experiment in the same way. She was definitely not interested and felt shocked that he even entertained the idea. Shortly afterward, while she was visiting her family in Michigan, David responded to newspaper ads and began meeting other gay men. After Joni's return home, David became more and more distant. "I confronted him February 3rd—there was some feeling he was pulling himself away from me emotionally. We went to bed angrier without resolving it. I cried because I didn't know what was happening. He was coming home later and he wasn't as attentive to me or my needs as he used to be. I dragged the truth out of him after crying and telling him that for better or for worse—I'd be there for him and we'd work things out just fine. I just wanted to know the truth. I didn't want to be in the dark."

Joni then learned that David had been ambivalent about his sexuality for a long time, but had not explored it before. He is the youngest of nine children in a Catholic family. When he was eleven years old, one of his sisters came out as a lesbian. Joni believes that he repressed his own homosexuality for so many years because of the havoc caused by his sister's disclosure. But after two years of marriage, he became clearer about himself and acted on his homosexual impulses. "He explained how he feels when he meets with this guy and how different he feels when he's with me. With me he's in control of his emotions, but with him, he's not." Once again, specific, unusual actions started the chain of events leading to a gay husband's disclosure.

Getting Honest

As these diverse examples illustrate, many homosexual husbands leave clues about their true identity, sometimes for years before they come out. It almost seems that they want their orientation to be discovered by their wives, avoiding the pain of putting the truth into words. There is a gradual buildup to disclosure—perhaps a cache of homosexual magazines discovered in the bedroom or the sudden development of new, single friends. My husband Jim abruptly became passionate about volunteer work with our city's AIDS Project. Without prior experience in gay rights work, he volunteered in the office, joined the board, acted as treasurer for the organization, and became a major donor. Why the sudden interest in this particular cause? Such a buildup of unusual actions brings growing tension and confusion in the family, often marked by withdrawal, coldness, and friction. Perhaps these husbands leave clues because they fear telling the truth, thus inducing even more guilt and anxiety.

Clearly, there is no painless way for a gay husband to come out to his wife. But the most negative cases seem to be the most abrupt. There is deliberate deceit, often for years, with no fidelity or honesty, followed by an explosion of truth. Wives of these men—like Betty and Andrea—are more vulnerable to a crisis of grief, similar to the crisis following a death in the family.

Regardless of the nature of a gay husband's disclosure—whether brutal or kind—it is clear that his wife's life is forever changed. Her response to this shocking new reality will largely determine her future. How she reacts, both immediately and through the days and years following, will color the rest of her life. The next chapter will explore some wives' actions after discovering their husbands' homosexuality.

3

Initiation into
The Closet

Few of the women I interviewed left their marriages immediately after they learned of their husbands' homosexuality. A small number hoped for some reversal that would allow a return to their earlier relationship with their men. Some fashioned alternative contracts to salvage some vestige of the marriage. Others were too devastated to move; some sank into depression in various forms; and some were trapped by financial considerations. Though their situations differed enormously, almost all remained in the home, working through their early reactions in secret. For many, the cycles of emotion and recognition lasted only days or weeks before they decided to leave. Others took much longer to process their decision to separate. But for those who chose to remain with their husbands after disclosure, the closet became their home for years.

As I talked with more and more women, definite patterns of behavior emerged. Many of them used identical phrases to describe their initiation into their strange new life of secrecy. During the time they processed the implications of their husbands' revelations, nearly everyone experienced all the feelings described in this chapter, though not necessarily in the same sequence or with the same speed. Here is a look inside the secret, closeted existence of straight spouses.

Shock, Illness, Disorientation

Receiving the unexpected news that your husband is gay is a visceral experience. Some women's feelings are reminiscent of the effects of a horror movie—only this calamity is real. Joni described her first reaction. "Speechless, I immediately went to the bathroom and just gathered myself on the floor in a crouch position, hugging my knees and saying, 'No! This can't be happening to me!'"

Sarah described it similarly: "One night when I was in the house alone . . . I sat curled in a corner and screamed and cried for several hours. (I thoroughly spooked the cat!) I wanted to be somewhere where I'd never heard of the term homosexual."

Shock and disbelief are the most common first reactions. Susan, for example, was the last in her immediate family to realize the truth. Here is how she learned about her husband, Roger, after thirty-five years of marriage. "In 1993 he began losing weight and I became concerned. I asked him to please go to a doctor. He told me it was not a physical, but a mental problem. He then told me about the young man he was involved with who was thirty-four. Our son was thirty-three at the time! To say the least, I was shocked and hurt. I kept it from our kids for nine months, trying to work with him, but finally they came to me because of *my* weight loss and said they knew something was wrong. They wanted to know what it was. Finally, my daughter asked, 'Is Dad having a homosexual affair? Really, Mom, you always took us to the Little League activities and had the car fixed, and Dad would take me shopping for my clothes and stuff to decorate the house.' Strange how others can see it and you can't."

Bonnie also reported that her immediate reaction to the truth was disbelief. "About three days after my husband's disclosure I ended up in the hospital with a bleeding ulcer. And the second reaction was to become literally ill—in my whole sense of being.

"I'd been unable to sleep and/or eat properly, so would get up in the mornings with a terrible headache. I'd take two aspirin—not knowing I was allergic to them—and drink them down with coffee. No thought of food! Four hours later, I'd take two more aspirin. When I was vomiting blood, I called the school and my husband came home and rushed me to the hospital…. A day and a half later, I had surgery at 2:00 A.M., as they couldn't get the bleeding to subside. I had eight pints of blood and it scared my husband beyond belief."

Here is another example of a physical reaction. Depressed after Beth gave up hope for the relationship, she contracted a stubborn laryngitis that lasted for two months, a great detriment to her work as a teacher. She now believes that the laryngitis was symbolic of her unsettled state and utter disorientation at the time. In a psychological, as well as a physical sense, Beth lost her voice.

Betty's health was the most fragile of all those I interviewed. Since her husband came out to her and abruptly left her, she has suffered from hypertensive diabetes, a heart attack, and now a terminal immune system disorder. Who can prove that there is a direct cause-effect relationship? But the fact is that Betty held a responsible job as a nurse/administrator until her husband came out. "I went from a valued employee to an unemployed, disabled, uninsurable, welfare mother," she sighed. "Now I'm dependent on food stamps and Section 8 housing!"

Meanwhile, after the wife has become aware of the truth, life outside the marriage must go on as before—on the surface. While a straight spouse struggles to make sense of her husband's homosexuality, she has to maintain some semblance of a normal routine. It is necessary to continue everyday responsibilities, even as the whole earth is moving underfoot.

Hiding behind a thin façade is disorienting to people not accustomed to secrecy. An entry from my journal illustrates. "Sleep came—blessedly—after Sunday unfolded as a fragile, teary time. I was pretty dysfunctional at the office today, avoiding contact and conversation. People chalked it up to my dad's worsening leukemia, so I didn't have to explain. I had another appointment with my friend, now my therapist, Deb. It was an enormous relief to pour out the surrealistic events of this week to a professional listener. Despite yesterday's trauma, I was amazed at my clarity today. I felt better after the session and even went back to work to complete a minor project at my desk."

While appearing to carry on as usual, women in this situation recognize a recurring sense of disoriented groundlessness.

Relief

"I thought, 'Whew, then it's not me!'" These very words were repeated in most of my interviews. After the first shock wave of disclosure, there is another common secondary emotion: relief. Most of the women I interviewed had known for a while (sometimes for years) that something was amiss in their marriage. Most of them also concluded that their husbands were gay because they themselves were somehow inadequate. When Daniel told Carlotta, her strange reaction was laughter! She thought, "It wasn't me," and felt overwhelming relief.

Over and over, I heard the same idea expressed. I experienced it too. We all thought that if we were prettier, or sexier, or thinner, or smarter, or richer, or a better cook, or more clever, or more witty, our husbands would love us more. Maya expressed it well. "There were many times during our thirteen-year marriage when I thought if only I could do it his way, everything would be all right. It never worked. Having almost no sex life with my husband during my thirties was certainly hard on my self-esteem. Being in a destructive relationship, whatever the cause, has to take its toll on both people and we both suffered."

After learning the truth about their husbands, it isn't surprising that these wives were flooded with an odd relief. It wasn't their problem after all. Sarah's feelings were similar, though her sense of inadequacy was more focused. "My eighteen-year marriage was based on love, friendship, and trust. It was a happy and mutually supportive relationship with shared goals and interests. It was physically close, but not passionate. About five years prior to Tim's telling me he was gay, I was very concerned about the sexual side of our marriage. Tim did not initiate sex—we would sometimes go two or three months without sex. When I would initiate it, we'd carry it through, but often he was unable or unwilling. We would cuddle and go to sleep in an embrace. Each summer I would go to Canada to a family cabin. I would be gone about a month, always hoping for a passionate reunion. We'd be happy to be together again, but there was only a lukewarm physical joining, or none at all.

"We made a decision together that Tim would take a job with an oil company in Saudi Arabia. We rented our house, packed all our belongings, and headed for what we hoped would be a lifetime adventure and a chance to renew our relationship. Tim became very distant during the process of preparing to go and explained that he was just preoccupied with the details and responsibilities of moving his family to the other side of the world.

"Unknown to me, he had confided to a new friend that he was struggling with his homosexual feelings. This had occurred while I was in Canada, saying goodbye to my family. Once in Saudi Arabia, he became even more distant. I was feeling very isolated and suspected all manner of horrors, but I was unwilling to confront him with my fear that he was gay. I finally couldn't stand the tension and, on my knees in a house in the desert of a foreign land, I asked him to tell me what was wrong. I'd known and loved him for so long, but felt I was with a stranger.

"Tim said he didn't love me anymore, and he needed time away from me to think about what he was going to do. We stayed in Saudi Arabia for six weeks and then packed our things and headed home. If there is such a thing as hell, those six weeks were it for me.

"My son and I lived with friends until we could get back into our house. Tim moved to an apartment. We were apart about five months when Tim came to me and said that whatever it was he was trying to get away from, it wasn't me. He wanted to come back home.

"After nine months of being back together, I still strongly suspected that Tim was gay. I confronted him and he broke down and said the homosexual feelings he had had since he was a pre-teen would not go away. There were times in our marriage when he thought he had overcome them, but they kept coming back."

"Before I knew about Tim's homosexuality, I blamed myself for not being attractive or sexy enough to turn my husband on. It was not a total self-esteem issue; it was very specifically sexual."

Beth succinctly summarized the self-doubt that led to the relief most of my interviews revealed. "If I were enough, this would work."

Feeling Stupid

The initial relief many women described was soon joined by other emotions. I wondered, "How could I have lived with a gay man for all these years and not know?" I felt especially stupid when I learned that most of our employees knew long before I did. A few months after Jim moved to his new house, a long-term woman employee invited me to a football game. We were friends in a professional sort of way. I was still being very discreet about the reasons for my separation from Jim. As we chatted about many things driving to the stadium, she abruptly said, "Carol, everyone at the office knows." I was taken completely by surprise. She related that a former employee, who was openly gay, had seen Jim at a Denver bathhouse—a center for homosexual encounters— and had whispered about it at the office. The incident had happened several years before. Many of the people at work knew about Jim's clandestine activity, but they pretended ignorance to protect me. My friend told me this with kindness, feeling that I ought to be aware of how many people already knew about Jim's actions. Nevertheless, I was not only embarrassed—I felt really stupid.

Andrea's discomfort was more acute. "I had lost self-esteem by being in a loveless, sexless sham of a marriage for nine years. He had worn me down with criticism and by being unavailable to me. There was an aspect of shame and feeling stupid that I had been fooled for so many years."

For months or even years after disclosure, it is common for straight spouses to second-guess themselves in this way. But they are not really stupid, of course. They have simply been misled.

Suicidal or Self-Destructive Action

Their immediate sense of betrayal becomes nearly unbearable for women who had no prior suspicion of their husbands' orientation. The initial shock quickly changes to deep hurt over their loss of trust. Sooner or later, the pain of betrayal leads many women to self-destructive behavior. Violence, suicide, alcoholism, and drug abuse are possible dangers. Anything to escape their anguish.

Alice's disclosure crisis was swift and intense. When her husband moved out for two months for no apparent reason, she suspected that he was having an affair with another woman. She was already quite depressed when he returned home and told her the truth about his homosexuality. Alice was utterly shocked. "We talked about his being gay for hours, and then he went to bed and I went out to the garage and tried to commit suicide in our minivan. I tried several times to kill myself after that, and later committed myself to the psychiatric ward at the hospital. I didn't blame myself, but I had very low self-esteem. I thought that I must be a very unattractive person to have kept a gay man happy for all those years."

Suicidal thoughts like this were common among the women I spoke with. One study suggests that probably fifty percent of the wives in this situation are at high risk for suicide at some point in their journey. Perhaps one-third make an actual attempt to end their lives.

Other women don't take such extreme action, but over time may fall into a slower form of self-destruction with alcoholism or other substance abuse. Katie, for example, drifted into alcoholism. She was overcome by anger and hurt. "We lived a lie because of my inability to face losing my best friend—the person who brought me to life, made life fun, and buffered me from its adversities. Of course, all the while our relationship was chipping away at my already precarious self-esteem."

Katie had begun to suspect that her husband was gay after they had been married four years. "We had two daughters, but I knew something was wrong sexually." She confronted the issue by asking if he thought he was a latent homosexual. He vehemently denied it. "We stayed married another nine years, the truth becoming more evident by the year with no discussion or admission. Finally I divorced him"

During the next seven years, their relationship was bitter. In her despair, Katie drank more and more heavily and finally became a serious alcoholic, spending time in a treatment center to work on her alcohol abuse and co-dependency. She was fortunate to survive and has been dry for seven years now. Experiences like these are common in this group of women, growing from their inevitable depression after learning the truth about their husbands' sexual orientation.

Increased Intimacy

Sharing a secret of this magnitude may create a bond of sympathy and compassion, particularly in the first days after disclosure. This is especially likely where there has been a good measure of mutual love and respect in the marriage. For example, after Daniel told Carlotta the truth, they spent a weekend in the mountains in deep discussion about their past and possible future. Carlotta began to understand Daniel's nervous breakdown as a college freshman and his attempted suicide. He had been advised to suppress his homosexual urges by a therapist, which he managed to do for many years. Though their spiritual bond was firm, they confirmed that their marriage was over that weekend. They worked deliberately together for nearly four years after that preparing for their eventual separation and amicable divorce.

In my case, there was a dizzying mixture of hope, hurt, and despair, but I desperately wanted our marriage to hold together. My idealism prevailed for a while. In my journal I wrote, "Where from here? My mind reels with the magnitude of this change, but my heart clings to the hope that we can grow beyond our wounds and build a new, truthful relationship. It's clear that we both want to have some kind of life together, but what a bizarre marriage this has become.

"Is a lifetime bond possible, despite our vast differences? The odds are against it, but we have been astonished this weekend at the closeness we suddenly feel. Jim's tears washed away years of secrecy and shame. With his truthfulness this weekend and his solemn promise to continue telling only the truth, Jim has risen, not fallen, in my esteem. This in itself is a miracle.

"For now, then, our plan is to continue counseling jointly and separately to help us adjust to this revelation. Though at this moment I feel no resentment, I fear my anger will build. Will I begin to feel cheated, antagonistic? Will judgment raise its ugly face? Will my present warmth toward Jim turn cold? The path ahead is rocky and shrouded in uncertainty. All I know tonight is that I want to heal my marriage."

My first blush of optimism lasted only several days. Later in the following week, I clung to the hope that truthfulness was a lasting possibility for us. I felt genuine compassion for Jim's life-long necessity to live a lie. "Truth cleanses. After Friday night's catharsis, this weekend took on a closeness Jim and I have not known ever before. His anguished confession did indeed set us free to relax a little and explore meanings. We rested in each other's acceptance.

"So many questions were answered. Remembered hurts, the enigma of Jim's aloofness, his frequent absences, his flamboyant young friends—it all makes sense now. We talked again and again about his experiences with male sex partners. How sad that all were anonymous except three. Intimacy with a nameless stranger must surely be the abyss of loneliness.

"Perhaps this unaccustomed truthfulness allows us the possibility to build a genuine life together, giving us understanding unknown in our old, separated compartments. I'm overwhelmed with thankfulness for this second chance to have the kind of companionship I've only dreamed about, even if that relationship is asexual. Even if our marriage is different from most, perhaps it can still be solid and loving.

"The other sensation I feel is fatigue. I am very tired physically, as though I'm recovering from a long, debilitating illness. This will pass I'm sure. In the meantime, I intend to take care of myself the best I can—good food, less alcohol, lots of rest, massage. This past year has been the most difficult of my life. May the loneliness and separation begin to heal now."

As much as I tried to sustain it, however, the glow of our new-found intimacy lasted only a short while.

Curiosity About Gay Lifestyle

While some of the women I met avoided knowledge of any detail of their husbands' gay activities, many became intensely curious. Carlotta, for example, worked hard at learning all about homosexuality, at least from an intellectual standpoint. After Daniel said, "I think I'm gay," they decided to research the subject together, spending a lot of time learning about what the word gay means. True to their academic background, the two shared books and discoveries. They learned together in a very intentional way.

I wasn't that organized. I simply bombarded Jim with questions in those raw days after his surprise announcement. I saw that my husband, whom I thought I knew and understood so completely, had led a double life for many years. His first encounters with other men occurred while we lived in Portland when he was twenty-three or twenty-four. He was initiated, ironically, through a gift from me. I gave him a membership at the downtown YMCA to help him stay fit. He found a hotbed of gay sexual activity there and participated in it for the first time. Though he had known earlier that he preferred men, his fears and conservative upbringing caused him to suppress his feelings, hardly admitting them even to himself. For the first time, I began to understand his habitual aloofness. I wrote in my journal, "He explained that he'd survived thirty years of a heterosexual marriage, fathering our two sons and fulfilling the image expected of him by completely compartmentalizing his two personas. Both of his images were real, and he had to switch from one identity to another again and again. He had to bury his emotions. It was the key to his survival. With our family, he was the traditional father and husband, albeit somewhat distant. When he traveled on his own, he cruised gay bars and bathhouses in many cities, finding sex when he got lucky with anonymous partners. In truth, he was emotionally disconnected from everyone—not just from me."

I began to understand his "wall" that I was always aware of but never able to climb. For years I begged Jim to let me into his life, to let me share his thoughts. Now I know that the more I pushed, the harder it was for him to be close to me; he thought, probably correctly, that I couldn't stand the truth. Carrying his heavy secret, he hid from me emotionally, consciously driving me away these past few months while he built his determination to become more authentic and live the gay life—his natural identity.

My curiosity raged, especially at first. Since I knew absolutely nothing about homosexual activities, I pressed for information. Here are some excerpts from my journal during that time. "It has been two days since this turn of fate. For the rest of the Memorial Day weekend, we talked constantly, all day and in the middle of the night. I couldn't get enough information. I asked hundreds of questions. My curiosity about his foreign lifestyle was insatiable. Jim patiently and completely answered every question, though he was sometimes embarrassed.

"How do you find out which places are gay bars?"

"What do you say?"

"How do you know someone else is gay—how can you tell in a crowd?"

"What did you do in those bathhouses?"

"How does it feel when a man touches you?"

Once, when I doubted his claim that he could locate the gay community in any city, he responded by looking up the Gay and Lesbian Community Center in the Denver white pages. He told me that most major cities have such listings. He dialed the help line and I listened in fascination as he said that he was in Denver on a business trip and was staying at the downtown Marriott. He inquired about friendly places near the hotel, writing down addresses of two bars and a bathhouse. His voice was different on the phone—a chatty, soft, intimate purr. I had never heard him speak that way. As he hung up, he handed me his notes and simply smiled.

Fear

Fear is inevitable, not just once, but many times. The women I spoke with feared AIDS, sexually transmitted diseases, loneliness, financial need, loss of security, destruction of the family, and the uncertain future. Some, like Betty, feared physical violence.

Andrea reported terror and panic when the workmen found her husband's cache of homosexual pornography, sex toys, and transgender clothing. During the next months, she spent "a lot of time in therapy, generally being anxious and frightened of this stranger I was married to." When she discovered his secret, she started plotting a way to escape the marriage safely and got an AIDS test." Her greatest fear was finding other unpleasant secrets because she couldn't trust him at all. She was afraid to ask for a divorce, "He has a bad temper and I believed he was capable of violence. I was pretty paranoid."

Many of the gay husbands also experienced fear. When Tim came out to Sarah, remorse and anxiety overcame him. "He cried for over an hour and I cried with him. He said he never stopped loving me and regretted the words spoken in Arabia, but he had felt it was an acceptable explanation for the way he was treating me then. He thought I would throw him out, stop loving him, if he told me the truth and he couldn't face that. He really didn't want to lose me and his son. My immediate reaction was fear for the end of the life I had known and enjoyed. I also needed to comfort and reassure Tim that my love for him was not a fickle thing."

Loss of a couple's familiar lifestyle was a common fear. Did this disclosure mean an abrupt ending of the life they had built together? Kaye's unusual experience of impending doom, related in an earlier chapter, occurred long after disclosure, after she and Joseph had established their alternative agreement to salvage their marriage. Her anxiety attacks, with racing pulse and inability to breathe, were brought on by the fear that Joseph was about to leave her.

Kaye reported one other occasion of cold fear, probably a year after her other anxiety attacks. Joseph had moved back home after a six-month absence during which he lived with his male lover. She and Joseph talked freely about his experiences in accepting his homosexuality and his difficulty in leading a double life. "On one occasion, he said he was trying to figure out what to do about it. I told him I'd just as soon he'd come out and let the chips fall where they might. He didn't take much to that and the conversation shifted to something else. However, I could tell over the ensuing weeks that he was mulling something over and I began fantasizing that he was about to come out and choose his lover over me. I knew I'd suggested it and should be courageous enough to accept what would come, but I was scared."

I shared many of the same fears after Jim came out, particularly after I began living alone. I had gone from my childhood home to a college dorm to my husband's home without ever living alone. Embarrassing as it is to admit, even in middle age I was afraid to stay alone at night.

While that fear lurked in the back of my mind, a more pressing one was the loss of sexual intimacy. "After feeling troubled all day, I was struck when I realized why. In our conversations about saving our marriage, Jim consistently expressed doubt regarding his ability to remain celibate. When he uses the word, he means, free of gay encounters. But when I hear the word I interpret it as without sex. Though we have made tender love once since Jim's revelation, it is depressing that he considers himself celibate. He merely goes through the mechanics of sex with me, though I know that he loves me as much as he can love any woman. God! Can this ever work?"

Underlying all my recurring fears was my old sense of inadequacy. A couple of weeks after Jim's disclosure, I had a significant, vivid dream—one of many that I recorded in my journal that summer. "I was going through stored decorative items—baskets, bottles, figurines, and small dishes. The idea was to bring these forgotten items back into usefulness, to fix them, clean them, restore them to the light. I wanted them to adorn our home. During this process, I was aware of Jim's presence, feeling uncertain in his cold gaze and hoping he'd approve of my using these old items as decoration."

I believe that the decorative pieces in the dream represent parts of myself, offered for Jim's approval. The containers hold love and compassion, ready to be poured out to save our relationship. The figurines are myself, offered to Jim. The house may represent our marriage and life together. Even in my sleep, I'm apparently trying very hard to make everything acceptable and even beautiful at home, but my fear of loss and failure is always just beneath the surface.

Plummeting Self-Esteem

Only a few of the women I interviewed said they did not suffer loss of self-esteem. For most women, their emotional roller coaster included a marked diminution of self-image. Most alternated between hope and despair, denial and regret, fear and calm. Their unsettled state rocked their confidence and sense of self. In the beginning, there was a kind of numbness that turned toward self-doubt and depression. Here is how it affected me. "I'm blocked. Haven't been able to write since Monday. I feel unbelievable fatigue, but it isn't fearful—only a quiet after struggle. I'm like a half-drowned swimmer dragged to the bank to pant and wheeze her gratitude for the rescue. Even the garden hasn't revived me. In normal times, I'm energized by the hard work there. Now I walk slowly among the trees, like one who has been seriously ill. I see the peonies and oriental poppies and even the spectacular giant allium as if I'm half-asleep. My physical reaction adds even more strangeness to this unique spring."

I found it hard to decide what to wear in the morning because I wasn't sure who I was anymore. Looking back at the few clothes I purchased then, it surprises me that they were so dowdy. They were loose, almost too big (I felt fat), and they were all made of dark-colored fabric. I took less interest in my general appearance for a long time.

Another symptom of my loss of confidence was the way I avoided contact with people. This was very difficult since I was in the staffing industry—people were my business. Another journal entry illustrates this. "Tonight Jim and I were trapped in one of those civic responsibilities one claims as part of business life. We were models for a charity fashion show to benefit WomenSource, a halfway facility for women recovering from drug and alcohol abuse.

One thing I most covet in retirement is an end to such participation—being 'on' in public. We were tied up most of the afternoon for last-minute fittings and an interminable makeup session. It took all my energy and determination to perform for 200 people, to pose and strut and be the epitome of confidence. It's all an act!

"I'm obsessed by the need to retreat—to think, feel, be, experience this particular time in my life. I'm afraid that I can't give enough love to keep Jim from choosing a male mate, but I have to let go of the temptation to cling. This reminds me of my self-talks when our sons were leaving the nest: 'The only way to hold onto a person's love is to let go of him.' I imagined a little bird in my hands, held there by interlocking fingers, then released to the freedom of the sky. This is so similar. The harder I hold on, the less chance our relationship has. "So I move another step away from the public persona, toward being simply myself. Probably by myself."

The women I interviewed echoed such self-doubts. Joni, who is a singularly beautiful young woman, was not exempt. She talked of her feelings when she first learned of David's orientation. "First, my self-esteem took a nosedive. I was crushed emotionally and physically. I felt so unattractive and useless. I had a hard time forgiving myself, but eventually with the help of therapy and modeling classes, I regained my self-confidence."

Laura, now in her mid-seventies and still married to her gay spouse, said she blamed herself and therefore lost self-respect. "Not knowing why he was acting the way he did made me question what I was or was not doing all the time. As a result, my self-esteem plummeted."

Annie, who married Jack knowing he was bisexual, described her feelings this way. "I felt impotent, a failure. I was unhappy. I didn't like who I was becoming in my frustration. There was no one to talk to. I should have known that I brought it on myself."

These comments are typical. Most of the women moved up and down the scale of self-confidence, usually alternating between a relatively healthy sense of self and the depths of self-deprecation. Sandy's account was interesting, offering a slightly different perspective. Her husband told her that he previously had one homosexual encounter before their marriage, so she was somewhat prepared when he moved further in that direction. She wrote, "I remember saying to a couple that I know, perhaps if I had been sexier, prettier, etc., we would still be together. The man said, 'Perhaps you are looking at the situation from the wrong angle. Perhaps you were a hell of a woman, keeping him straight as long as you did.' But of course I lost self-esteem. It is hard enough to see a man leave for another woman—but to leave for a man! I thought, in my irrational times, I must have been really horrible to cause him to change his sexual orientation." Such a negative self-image leaves a straight spouse vulnerable to desperate compromises, as she struggles to make sense of her new situation.

Attempts to Stay Married

Several of the women I met devised alternative marriage contracts in an attempt to remain married to their gay husbands. Five of my interviews were with wives who successfully stayed in their marriages for an extended period of time through determined, intentional agreements with their husbands.

Rita and Tom are among the most successful. Married nearly thirty years, they remain committed to each other. When Tom came out as a bisexual after eight years into their marriage, Rita's initial reaction was to ask him three questions:

"Do you still love me?"

"Do you still want to live with me?"

"Do you still want some type of physical/sexual relationship with me?"

"Without hesitation, when he responded enthusiastically to each question, we agreed to somehow make the relationship satisfying for both of us."

Such agreements usually involve a broad range of mutual promises, sometimes including a refusal to discuss homosexuality at all. Some couples hope to make homosexual tendencies go away by denying or ignoring their existence. One gay husband said, "My wife and I made an honest attempt to be dishonest" about the issue. Others discuss everything openly and repeatedly. Two of the women I met entered their marriages already aware of their husbands' homosexuality or bisexuality. Obviously, this prior knowledge gave them a completely different perspective from the women who were shocked by the news.

Cherie, who was mentioned previously, remains convinced that marriages like hers can work. Still in her late twenties, she and her husband were the youngest people I interviewed. Cherie feels enriched by her relationship with Roy, her bisexual husband, and has no intention of trying to change his affairs with men. They actually met each other in a gay bar. She insists, "If you fall in love with the person, why would you want to change him?" Cherie remembers that the only time she was seriously worried about Roy and their marriage was during the six months they lived in the Deep South. Because of prejudice and violence against gays there, Roy repressed his sexuality altogether. "He repressed his *real self*!" Cherie said. "He was *gone*. There was nothing left either for him or me."

Cherie and Roy are happiest when they both feel free to seek sexual companionship with others. They are even attracted to the same men! Their open marriage has worked for them since 1993, though they have sought counseling from time to time to get through temporary difficulties. Cherie attributes their success together to their mutual acceptance and "overriding truth, honesty, and communication." She also admits that she has always been regarded as a bit of a rebel and relishes pushing the edge of conventional behavior.

Zoe is the former actress who was also introduced in a previous chapter. Like Cherie, she was aware of her husband's bisexuality prior to their marriage. Zoe's approach, however, differs markedly from the openness described by Cherie and Roy. Instead, she and Charles don't discuss this issue. She describes him as a private person who was once planning to be a monk. "He's a nice man. He's defensive about his orientation—hasn't really come to terms with it." Though they have a minimal sexual relationship, their marriage is based more on friendship: "I'm his best friend," she says. Zoe has had one affair during their eight-year marriage, but does not know about Charles' extramarital activity. "I don't want to know. I would rather cover the truth."

When communication between them faltered, this determined couple decided to adopt a child. In their mid-forties, they now enjoy a lively three-year-old Chinese daughter. "Adopting a baby really helped our marriage by creating a community within the home," Zoe explains. Having a family has enhanced their closeness and their ability to talk meaningfully with each other. "We have something very important in common now."

When a mixed orientation couple chooses to remain married, their alternative contracts often involve denial of any pain and acceptance of little or no sex between them. Kaye is a good example. After thirty-six years, Kaye describes her present relationship with Joseph in this way. "We love each other very much and are committed to each other. We treasure the ongoingness of our marriage and family. Our relationship hasn't been as emotionally intense and close as it once was, but I think we're moving back toward that. I miss our sexual intimacy—even though it had its difficulties—but I can live with its absence. It's emotional distance and disconnection that I can't bear."

Still, she reported that the single thing that made her most angry was the fact she hadn't bargained for the loss of their sexual intimacy. Though her marriage and her hope continue, her path isn't easy.

Bonnie also extended her marriage for many years by creating a new agreement with her bisexual husband, Stan. Stan felt terrible about her bleeding ulcers and took full responsibility for it. A week after Bonnie was released from the hospital, still struggling with the shock of Stan's disclosure, a timely opportunity opened. The minister of their church and his wife were going to lead a six-week Marriage Group. Bonnie saw promise in it, though the other couples were straight, and she and Stan attended. The group bonded, shared deeply, and continued to support each other for years afterward. Bonnie wrote, "It was a meaningful experience and enabled each couple to see that what they experienced wasn't unique, but shared by the others. Stan and I privately decided we wanted to be married and we wanted to be married to each other; but if he ever wanted to relate to a man, he had to be honest with me and with himself. This agreement gave us another fifteen years of married life—which Stan claims to have enjoyed greatly."

About ten years after Bonnie and Stan made their decision and joined the couples' group, they began family counseling with one son who was having trouble communicating and relating and following their rules. Afterward, they continued counseling as a couple and Stan shared his fear of feeling attracted to men." This courageous pair persevered for years afterward.

Eventually, however, Bonnie's fears were realized. "For as long as my husband chose to be married, it couldn't have been a better marriage. He chose not to act upon that dimension of his life. Our sex life was very satisfactory (plus!), and we enjoyed being together. Things were meaningful and challenging and rewarding as we encouraged and delighted in each other—until he met his male soul mate. It was then he wanted to no longer be married."

Bonnie and Stan were married for twenty-eight years, then lived separately in the same house for one year longer. Bonnie describes her marriage as ideal for much of its duration. She emphasizes that their success in staying together was based on Stan's long-term choice not to act on his homosexual tendencies. The marriage ended when he could no longer repress those tendencies.

A straight wife's initiation into her gay husband's closet is a momentous event. These common responses indicate the breadth of the woman's trauma. When her husband's private closet door opens and the wife enters, she knows that her life will never be the same again.

4

Facing
New Realities

The last chapter described straight wives' early reactions to their husbands' disclosure of homosexuality: shock, relief, curiosity, fear, and despair. These were their initial responses, which alternated and repeated with varying impact for the first few days or weeks after they learned the truth. Once the initial shock subsided, however, a deeper understanding of the situation began to emerge. Sooner or later, these women faced challenging new realities about their predicament.

The foremost reality was the hardest—and the simplest: A homosexual man is married to a heterosexual woman and their disparate, innate sexual orientation will never change. Clinical professionals estimate that about one-fifth of straight wives cling to the hope that their gay husbands will somehow change and go back to their former, familiar marital patterns. These women want to believe that homosexuality is a choice, not a genetic characteristic. Sarah, for example, went with Tim to his counselor. "Tim asked the person to give him drugs, shock therapy, anything to make it go away. He was told that was not possible. The counselor gave us the best advice that finally let us get on with the

He said, 'If you want it to go away, you can turn
[...] my office now, because that can't be done. But
help you deal with it and find answers to what
[...]ow, have a seat.' I got separate counseling and basi-
[...] heard the same thing. 'Tim can't change; what are you going
to do about it so you can be happy and fulfilled?'"

Thus the hope that it will just go away usually wanes and with-
ers. Slowly, the impact of disclosure becomes clear. He will never
again be a conventional spouse; this marriage will never return to
its prior state. Even if the man is bisexual, even if he loves and is
attracted to his wife, he will also continue to be attracted to other
men. Both partners' understanding of their marriage must change
irrevocably. With this revised understanding as a foundation,
what other new realities does the wife begin to comprehend?

Marriage As His Cover

Andrea told me when we talked, "My husband knew he was gay
even before we were married. He decided to marry me and use
me as his cover. That's the issue. It's deception, betrayal, and lies.
It shows utter contempt."

A really degrading realization for a straight spouse is when she
realizes that the marriage served as a cover for his covert homosexual activities. Granted, this may not be his primary reason for
entering or staying with the covenant, but it certainly is a convenience while he remains in the closet. And it may be a political
or career necessity for him to stay with that cover. As discussed in
chapter one, the superficial public appearance of "the perfect couple" protects the husband's real sexual orientation. When this
becomes clear to his wife, she usually feels undervalued and
betrayed.

For months after Jim came out to me, we thought we could rebuild our former marital relationship. This struggle created a dilemma for us both. We were increasingly certain that he would not be able to resist other men. It was summertime, and Jim spent more and more time with his male friends. He took more trips out of town and I spent more time alone. I had a deep sense of dislocation and isolation. I was scared for us both. After painful consideration, I took a leap and offered him the gift of my consent. I wrote in my journal, "Since we are both certain that Jim will again act on his homosexual urges, I gave him my blessing to satisfy those needs outside our marriage, with only two conditions: Practice only safe sex and tell me no lies. We'll have no games, no recrimination—just honesty. He agreed to stop cruising gay bars and to swear off momentary encounters in toilets with strangers. Those practices are just too dangerous—for both of us. Jim showed increasing relief as we talked. He can have it all now, protected socially by the cover of a traditional-looking marriage."

A common response, according to the women I interviewed, was to decide that if the man could play around, then the woman could as well. "After all, it's the new millennium. Women have rights and freedom. We can play that game too." When Jim first came out to me, I found myself calling male friends and saying, "How about a drink after work?" We would meet, end up talking business, and I would hurry home embarrassed and completely insecure.

Kaye gave me an even more poignant example. Consumed with loneliness and feeling left out of Joseph's life, she decided to go out and see if she could enjoy a night on the town on her own. On a Saturday night, she dressed up in her favorite cocktail dress and went to a downtown hotel's best restaurant. The upscale place was well known as a popular spot for a romantic dinner and dancing. She thought that she might meet someone and enjoy an exciting evening out. Instead, Kaye said that she was seated at an undesirable table where she felt very conspicuous. She ordered her dinner, read a book while she ate, and—feeling acute embarrassment—retreated as soon as possible. Her despair over that awful evening was unspeakable.

This whole situation is humiliating and demeaning for most straight spouses. "How could he be this unfair to me?" is the central question. Middle-aged and older women who have been married a long time articulated their deepest hurt and sense of entrapment by being used as a cover. Vera, the wife of the expelled Air Force officer, is another good example. For that matter, so am I. The era of our upbringing made it much more difficult to go out while still married, as our husbands had long been doing—even if they urged us to try it. Indeed, as Kaye and I learned, we didn't even know how to begin.

Related Health Risks

When a straight spouse realizes how risky her home life is—depending upon the nature of her husband's outside sexual activity—she usually hurries to a medical clinic or public health center for an AIDS test. Rightly so. She may been exposed to HIV or other sexually transmitted diseases and should immediately ascertain her own state of health.

For any woman who has lived with a gay man, the importance of AIDS testing cannot be overstressed. While none of the women I interviewed have so far contracted these diseases from their husbands, most have been fearful about it. Like Carlotta, who decided that their marriage was over at the time of Daniel's disclosure, many had no further sexual contact with their mates. But those who continued to have unprotected sex for months or years after disclosure were clearly in jeopardy. I took the chance with Jim though I wouldn't do it again, for even during the time we were trying to save our marriage, we were both certain that his true homosexual nature would not be suppressed for long.

AIDS is still a major threat, even though recently developed anti-viral drug treatments have significantly reduced the number of deaths among people who already had the infection. These "drug cocktails" that include protease inhibitors decreased the AIDS death rate in the United States from a high of 49,985 in 1995 to 21,909 in 1997. That's good news, but the AIDS epidemic has not really abated; sick people are simply living longer because of the new drugs. More than 600,000 cases of AIDS have been reported in the United States since 1981, and as many as 900,000 Americans may be infected with HIV. Government statistics suggest that the annual number of *new* AIDS cases in the United States each year—about 40,000—has not declined in a decade.

Moreover, it is increasingly documented that unsafe sex is again on the rise among gays, who have a false sense of security because of the falling AIDS death rates. Younger men particularly have adopted a cavalier or even defiant attitude about condom protection. Epidemiologists expect HIV transmission to increase dramatically as a result. Numerous reports indicate both increased risky sex and increased illness among gays. Here are some statistics.

- The number of gay men who reported having unprotected anal sex went up from 35% in 1994 to 52% in 1997. (University of California, San Francisco)

- Of 2,543 gay men surveyed in seven cities, 30% reported having unprotected sex, and 7% of them were HIV positive. (Center for Disease Control)
- Two-thirds of gay men surveyed in Chicago, Denver, and San Francisco said they had unprotected sex at least once in the last 18 months. (Report to 1998 World AIDS conference in Geneva)

Richard Elovich, Director of Prevention for the Gay Men's Health Crisis, commented on these dangerous new attitudes about safe sex: "Simple-minded slogans—such as 'use a condom every time'—have become invisible, like the surgeon general's warning on the cigarette pack."

Another sobering fact is that HIV constantly is evolving into new strains, even as researchers labor to develop drugs and therapies to fight known ones. It is therefore very difficult to combat this genetically flexible human immunodeficiency virus. The World Health Organization estimated that there would be about 40 million AIDS cases, caused by innumerable HIV strains, by the year 2000.

AIDS is not the only danger, either. The U.S. Centers for Disease Control report that rectal gonorrhea increased significantly among gay men in the mid-1990s, more than doubling among those tested at clinics in Seattle and San Francisco. This is just one example of the rise in sexually transmitted diseases. These and other health risks are obvious for any wife who continues sexual contact with her gay husband.

These risks are not limited to the young, either. Though many studies like some noted here have focused on younger gay men, older Americans are not exempt from the trends. Just because a man comes out in later life, he and his wife are still susceptible to these dangers. In fact, patients older than fifty account for more than 10 percent of AIDS cases in the United States. And that number is increasing dramatically. Between 1991 and 1996, new cases of AIDS among people older than fifty rose 22 percent, compared with only a 9 percent increase for those younger than fifty.

Clearly, one of the burdens a straight spouse must bear is her own health, as well as worrying about her gay husband's health. Even if neither of them contracts a dangerous disease, the grief and strain of daily life takes its toll. Three months after Jim told me the truth, I wrote the following short passage in my journal. "This strange summer is nearly past. Life is hard for me. Writer's block. Deep grief. Recurring fear about my future with Jim. A severe attack of arthritis. Fatigue—bone tired most of the time. I long for a full night's sleep, but it doesn't come. These are the harsh parts of knowing." Health risks are multi-layered, encompassing emotional and psychological states, as well as the more obvious physical conditions.

Religious and Moral Conflicts

Moral and religious conflicts are another painful reality for such women. This is particularly true for those brought up in conservative religions or strongly moralistic homes. Lying, telling half-truths, and keeping guilty silence are daily necessities in the closet. Torn between their convictions and the required cover-up, they suffer greatly from shame and guilt. Yet family and outside life must be maintained as usual over this pervasive undercurrent of untruth. It is rightly said that secrets are like a silent cancer, eating away our souls. Entering a contract of secrecy with a gay husband erodes a wife's self-esteem and destroys her sense of authenticity.

Virtually all the women I spoke to talked of the pain of living with lies. It was the most difficult reality of all for me, because my highest aspiration was and still is personal authenticity. Particularly wounding was my inability to talk plainly and openly with my mother, who had always been my confidant. The situation forced me to dodge her questions and play games of secrecy—and I hated every minute of it. I also felt very guilty about hiding the truth from her and my sons and everyone else.

Kaye's years of shielding her two children from knowledge of their father's sexual orientation brought her an additional common heartache. Kaye knew of Joseph's orientation from the time their son and daughter were eight and twelve years old. Only recently were they told the family secret. When they were finally told the truth, their daughter reacted with enormous anger, directed primarily at Kaye. She was furious because she hadn't been told sooner, and because her brother knew before she did, and generally because she had been part of the big lie. Many months later the young woman, still alienated and angry, was seeing a therapist trying to resolve her negativity and confusion. The whole family suffers from the effects of secrecy.

If the straight spouse's religious tradition judges homosexuality wrong or sinful, this adds even more weight to her burden. Her whole lifestyle would be subject to censure if it were discovered. Moreover, her homosexual husband would be personally condemned by these beliefs. Religious organizations have been rocked by controversy about homosexuality for generations. Their teachings on the subject range from very liberal, allowing full participation of gays and lesbians in all aspects of religious life, to the most conservative which teach that homosexuality is a choice and a perversion which should be condemned as a sin against God. The debate goes on. Relevant here is the conflict this question creates in women who must keep the secret of their husband's homosexuality. Many straight spouses live in torment over these basic questions of ethics, values, and belief.

Wives are also impacted by their husbands' religious confusion. Betty's husband, for example, was brought up as a conservative Southern Baptist and felt very guilty. Such orientation was simply not acceptable. He therefore suppressed his sexuality for years, becoming ever more compulsive and neurotic, engaging in bizarre personal rituals and perpetuating the abusive behavior he'd experienced as a child. A few years after Betty divorced him, he converted to Mormonism at the urging of his brother and went to a Mormon therapist "to get over being gay." In his case two different fundamentalist religions, Baptist and Mormon, condemned his homosexuality with very negative impact on Betty and the family.

Sexual Repression

In a mixed orientation marriage, both partners experience sexual repression: the gay man because he's married, and the straight woman because she's married to a gay. Lack of sexual fulfillment is handled in various individual ways, some healthy and some not. A few specific examples will make the point.

Shortly after Jim came out to me, I wrote the following journal entry. "Masturbation: The stimulation of one's own or another's genitals to achieve orgasm. The dictionary definition is so clinical! I never thought much about it before. It's something everyone does and no one discusses. For me, it has been a rare to occasional decision, one that usually elicits guilt. To think that nearly all of Jim's sexual satisfaction in his entire life was from this act makes me terribly sad. For me, the orgasm comes, but it isn't very satisfying. It is a momentary physical rush, not an emotionally fulfilling experience. Sex means love to me. No separation. No compartmentalization. Our choice of words is significant. I say 'make love,' not 'have sex.' Poor Jim must have been even lonelier than I all these years."

My frustration was mild compared to Sandy's. Approaching middle age and longing to have a child, she was afraid that she would be too old to have a baby if she left James and started over. Hurt and angry over her husband's long history of deception and infidelity, she became frigid, unable to feel anything. During sex she would just check out and not be there emotionally. As she planned how and when she would leave their marriage, she reached a momentous decision—to use artificial insemination to become pregnant. Sandy later said, "My relationship with my ex-husband was like a hand of poker, in which I didn't have the winning cards."

That analogy applied to most of us. Vera wrote, "We just had a marriage of friendship." Kaye's poignant summary was, "I hadn't bargained for the loss of our sexual intimacy." Carlotta ended all sexual contact the night Daniel said, "I think I'm gay." Yet they lived together for another four years without sexual intimacy, protecting jobs and family, working toward divorce. Annie described her state with her bisexual husband as one of quiet desperation. She wrote, "I tried to interest him in sex with me in every way I could think of. He was unmovable."

In these mixed marriages, without doubt, both partners are repressed and frustrated. An essential part of life is missing for most of them.

My first clear realization of the depth of my frustration came through a vivid dream, which I related to my therapist and recorded in my journal the summer after Jim's Memorial Day disclosure. My father had died in early July that same summer. This was the dream. "I am at my parents' house, in the upstairs bedroom. I walk down the stairs into the living room and see my dad in his red plaid wool shirt and corduroys. He is mature, smiling, vibrant, healthy—as he was before the leukemia. He sees me also and is benign but detached. 'Daddy!' I cry, but he doesn't reply. As I move toward him, he walks slowly toward the other end of the long room. I follow him, holding my breath, not speaking. Then he turns left, toward the far side of the room, smiles back at me, and silently walks through the wall, out of my sight.

"At the same moment when my dad disappears, I see a Dark Lady. She is strikingly beautiful, with slightly graying black hair to her shoulders. She wears a black cape over a stylish, silken red dress. I am strongly drawn to her and move closer to see her more clearly. As I slowly come closer, she becomes vaguely sinister. And when I face her squarely, her appearance changes in a frightening way.

"I am terribly afraid, but can't move. We're close together—face to face. Suddenly, her mouth twists into a snarl, exposing vampire-like teeth. She grasps my left hand in her right. Her long red thumbnail deeply scratches the top of my hand. I see my blood and have a momentary panic that I am somehow infected by this strange being."

I woke up panting and sweating. I believe that the Dark Lady personified my own sexuality, which I had repressed in a quite conscious way since learning of Jim's homosexuality. I intellectualized everything in my entire life and reasoned that I could successfully sublimate and work off my sexual urges. I exercised, filled my schedule with volunteer and consulting work, traveled, read, meditated, and stayed constantly busy. The Dark Lady was both stunningly beautiful and dangerous to me. She had been suppressed for years—first because Jim had always kept his distance, and later because I avoided sex through fear of AIDS and because my knowledge of Jim's homosexuality was an emotional turn-off. The Dark Lady's bloody attack probably represents my fear of infection and the fact that I had repressed this part of my life for too long. I created a monster out of something natural and desirable.

Dread of Stigma

Most of the women I interviewed talked of their fear of discovery. They dreaded embarrassment or disgrace because of societal expectations. Their husbands' sexual orientation broke the code of the community's mores and they felt that they would be stigmatized, along with their husbands if people found them out. This fear was most pronounced among the older women in the group—Vera and Laura and Susan, for example—who were more grounded in the family values of the 1950s. Though he was homosexually active until he died with AIDS in 1985, Vera's husband never came out publicly and she never told any of her friends about his hidden life or cause of death. She keeps all their secrets to this day. This was a typical pattern. My conversations uncovered many such examples.

Personally, I was not so troubled by this fear of discovery, reasoning that we lived in a liberal, well-educated city that prides itself on its celebration of diversity. But that assumption was naïve. Even in such an environment, people did judge and whisper when Jim came out. I got the message clearly after my divorce when a man I went out with told me that his friends thought he was very brave to be with me. It shocked me when he said it in a kind but matter-of-fact way, "You know that *you* carry a stigma, too." Strange, it hadn't occurred to me until then. Guilt by association I guess. I had been foolish to think otherwise.

This dread of stigma is a major reason that some mixed couples decided to remain married. It appeared easier to stay together than to face the real or imagined horrors of society's judgment. As seventy-year-old Laura said, "In the winter of our lives, it seemed better to stay married."

Caring for the Children

Coping with their husband's sexual orientation was probably slightly easier for the women who had no children living at home at the time. They were able to adjust to this new knowledge with more space and privacy. How or whether to talk with children about the issue was a huge problem for many of the women I interviewed. Even for those whose children were grown and out of the nest, the dilemma of what and when to tell them became a burden.

Each couple approached this issue in their own way, depending upon the age of the children, their relationship to the parents, and their established family patterns. Each case was different, but a few examples may illustrate varied approaches.

Their three sons were very young—fourteen months, three, and six years old—when Bonnie first learned that Stan had a gay encounter with a friend of theirs. Her shock and subsequent hospitalization with bleeding ulcers were described in a previous chapter. Bonnie and Stan managed to reconcile and enjoy many meaningful years of marriage after that early discovery. Because they were working together to sustain their nuclear family and because the children were too young to understand the matter at the time, they kept their secret. They never considered telling the children or anyone else through the following fourteen years of their marriage. "We only told our family when we decided after twenty-nine years of being together that we would separate." That decision came when Stan met his male soulmate.

Their method of telling their now-grown sons was interesting. Bonnie and Stan each composed a letter relating their story and reasons for their decision to separate. They met first with their sons and their wives and read the letters aloud. They offered to answer any questions then or later. Afterwards, without delay they left the room, "so everyone would have time to talk to each other and recover from the unexpected news." They used the same letters and a similar plan to make the announcement to a group of their close friends at church.

Carlotta's children were eighteen and thirteen when Daniel told her he thought he was gay. While she and her husband explored their options and learned more about homosexuality in general, they chose not to tell the children anything about it. But six months later, after they had figured out what this meant for them, they explained the situation to the kids. They had a family meeting to talk it through. Sometime afterward, their son announced the facts to his whole police academy class, and their daughter told fifteen of her friends at a slumber party. (Carlotta confided that her daughter's worst fear was that her father's voice would change.) The relatively healthy way these young people responded was a tribute to their home environment and probably to their parents' training in education. This family was luckier than most, because they continue to maintain friendly ties even after the divorce. As Carlotta said, "The marriage is over, but the family still exists."

Not all the women fared so well. Annie knew before she was married to Jack that he was bisexual. She knew Jack never wanted children, but she was pregnant with their first child when they decided to get married. During the eight years they stayed together, she was increasingly frustrated by Jack's disinterest in sex. Angry and unfulfilled, she made an appointment with him to get pregnant with her second child. They were always open about Jack's orientation with their friends, but Annie worried that their sons would learn of it from other children in their small town. "I wanted Jack to talk to them first. I don't think he ever did," she says. There were repercussions. Though there wasn't real physical violence in their home, the general atmosphere was hostile. Annie remembers, "In my frustration, I did scream at him, and I may have hit him in a flailing, non-injurious way." The older son was eight when Annie and Jack separated. She reported that both boys were "badly damaged psychologically. Lots of unhappiness had surrounded them." They responded by pitting one parent against the other; later they had difficulty in school. The older boy suffered from depression and eventually became suicidal, though he is better now and in counseling.

Their second son, a very different personality, fared better over time. Annie said with obvious love, "He was 'born congruent,' and is chatty like a daughter. He's like the evolved Jack, with the same wisdom. They're so much alike." When the boy left home for his freshman year in college, she reported, "I'll miss my pal," Annie muses. "I've learned so much from my son."

Annie speaks thoughtfully of her private grief. "I'm sorry I had so few skills and knowledge. Our communication was so bad and we were poor models for our boys. I regret deeply the pain they experienced, seeing our bad behavior."

Caring for the health and well-being of children after disclosure adds a huge measure of stress to an already difficult time. Even in the best of these situations, there is great sadness. Sarah reports: "We were both very sad about the effect on our son because he was so bewildered. We had separated, gotten back together, and then had to tell him we were divorcing. He had rarely if ever seen us exchange harsh words or be unhappy with each other. He couldn't reconcile what was happening with what his experience told him about the strength of the relationship of his parents.

"Tim had a weekend with our son soon after we told him we were divorcing. Tim told him that he was gay. The response was, 'It's okay, Dad, I still love you.' The boy was relieved to finally have a valid reason for what was happening."

Facing these new realities is hard for the entire family.

Growing Sadness, Overwhelming Loneliness

All the realities in this chapter are interrelated. A straight spouse's realizations come and go, deepen and widen, as time passes and her initial shock wears off. Each of these insights occurs like an epiphany—a sudden flash of truth that was previously unclear. They accumulate, weigh down, layer after layer, creating growing sadness and a sense of monumental loss. All her former life plans have changed. All her dreams, hopes, and expectations are dashed. She will probably not grow old with this man she loved and married. Nothing will ever be the same in this lifetime. So the result of her layers of realization is immense disappointment. The center didn't hold.

Coupled with this sense of loss is overwhelming loneliness. Again and again, we all thought, "I'm the only one who has ever felt this way. I'm the only one." Translation: "I can't talk to anyone about this sorrow. No one can understand what I'm going through. There's nowhere to turn. I'm all, all alone in this terrible despair!" Eventually, many women are so overwhelmed by the accumulated stress they shut down emotionally, they become numb. When I experienced this stage, I felt almost like two people—a stranger who inhabited my dragging body, and a detached observer, watching the whole drama with dark fascination. But the numbness doesn't last forever. It leads to another, more active phase: anger.

5

The Black Hole

Anger is a secondary emotion. It is the aftermath of being hurt in some way. If we examine our feelings just prior to being angry, we find some other experience that served as its catalyst. In the last chapter we explored the raw realities that gradually settle on a straight spouse as days and months pass after her husband's disclosure. Sooner or later as a result of her wounded spirit she gets angry. While it can be a frightening experience, anger is actually good news—it means that the woman is making progressive steps toward eventual recovery. She has finally asked the key question, "What about me?" Like the stages of grief, established by the research of Elisabeth Kubler-Ross, the straight wife's journey to recovery is definable, and it definitely includes anger.

The stages of coping are fairly clear, though not every person experiences these steps in the same order, or with the same intensity. Some of the women I spoke with moved through all the common emotions very rapidly, while others took many years in their process—often repeating steps with different levels of experience. For them it was something like climbing a spiral staircase, going over and over the same ground, but on a different level each time. Because this journey is so extremely individual, dependent upon personality, values, environment, upbringing, education, sense of self, and other intensely personal factors, we will again rely on representative real-life experiences to define this necessary stage.

My own central emotion, after the stark reality of my situation became clear, was deep sadness. It came in great waves, ebbing and flowing like the tide. Everything Jim and I had accomplished together no longer counted; our bright future plans were never to be realized. We would not enjoy a peaceful retirement together. We would not travel the world together. We would not know the security of mutual, loving support. We would not grow old together in our cozy home. When this became depressingly clear, I experienced huge mood swings. I would cope pretty well for days at a time, then hit what I came to call a black hole. Each time another crisis struck, I experienced terrible despair, like a freefall into an abyss of terrifying darkness.

As an example, for weeks Jim and I had planned to go to the local dinner theater. Nervous to be going out with my own husband (now that I knew more about him), I wore my prettiest dressy outfit, a simple black dress with a gold paisley jacket. I spent extra time fussing with my hair and makeup. I wanted everything to be perfect that evening. (I suppose that I was still trying to impress or seduce him.) Everything seemed fine as we enjoyed dinner and a good performance of *Cabaret*.

But afterward, it wasn't so pleasant. I described the ordeal in my journal. "When we returned home, I was again abruptly overwhelmed by the sadness of our probable separation. I dropped into a black cave of desperate despair. I love Jim. I really don't want to lose him. But now it seems inevitable. Since this whole drama began, I have been afraid that if I ever let go of my tight hold on my emotions, if I ever start to weep, I might never stop crying. I've dammed up floods of tears.

"But I did let go last night. I cried bitterly all night. Everything I ever wanted is out of my grasp. Why? Why! My ribs ache today from those terrible, tearing sobs. My whole face feels raw. I hate this fearful uncertainty and pray that my radical moods will somehow level. I can't stand this ambivalence!"

Right after that particular emotional crash, Jim left with four men for yet another boating vacation at Lake Powell. On Monday, I was bombarded at work with decisions and responsibility I was supposed to share with him. I resented the fact that he was working only about half time and spending so many days playing at the lake. Why should I have to pick up the slack?

Midmorning, I attended graveside services for a friend's father, who had been an avid fisherman and outdoorsman. I was touched by sweet, homely eulogies by his old buddies, praising a man who was plain-spoken and simple like my own dad. I grieved for my friend and her father and for my father—and for myself.

Teary-eyed, I returned to the office where I immediately received a long-distance call from Jim. He phoned from Bullfrog Marina to say that he was having such a great time at the lake, he and the guys had decided to stay over another few days. I calmly hung up the phone, then exploded inside. Jim had it all and I did not! I was flooded with rage, thinking all Jim thought about was entertaining himself. Having fun, especially with 'the boys,' seemed like it was his top priority. It made me furious! That night, still in a rage, I wrote: "What is he bringing to the table in our attempt to heal? He confessed that he's gay. Is that his only responsibility? Is that enough? Now he's free to go about his unspeakable business without censure. Can he now run around with his queer buddies, blaming infidelity on his nature and feeling guiltless because I know? How much do I not know? He lied to me for thirty years. I had no clue that he was doing so. How can I trust him now?

"What do I have? I get the leftovers of his energy—at work, at home, in bed, on social occasions. I'm always second in line. Where does he get off thinking that because he told me the truth about being gay, he's suddenly exonerated, free to keep on with his swinging life, while his little bird at home waits under his table to peck up the crumbs? I'm hurt. I'm sad. I'm furious tonight."

Notice that sadness led to this particular bout of anger. Like kites, driven up and down by capricious gusts, Jim and I skittered through many months like this with alternate times of hope and despair, optimism and frigid fear—and inevitable anger. For us both, the closet was a lonely, discouraging trap. And my recurring black hole threatened my mental and physical health for years afterward.

Triggers for Rage

Virtually all the women I interviewed agreed that their situation was grossly unfair. Their loss of security and isolation in the closet led most to question, "Why me? What did I do to deserve this?" Feeling victimized, confused, and hurt, they experienced various triggers for the rage that followed.

Deception was the most commonly cited catalyst. We hated the thought that our husbands had lied to us for years in an intricate pattern of deception. Sandy was enraged because James promised to be faithful to her, then wasn't. At first, she was unsuspecting and maintained the stability of the marriage in good faith. "I was the warp on the loom and he wove in and out as he pleased," she said ruefully. His covert activity discovered, Sandy said, "The thing that made me most angry was when he used me to hide behind without my permission. We were the normal, happy couple on the surface, while he went out in secret."

Integrity was the major issue here and Sandy stayed very angry over this for a long time. A librarian by profession, she loves reading mystery books. Perhaps her fascination with stories of crime prompted the question, but at one point when she was most alienated, James asked her if she'd ever thought of murdering him. She replied, "No—if I'd wanted to kill you, you'd already be dead!" Now that she's beginning to recover her balance, Sandy believes that her rage hurt her much more than it did her husband, but it was a necessary component of her decision to end the marriage and start over.

Loss of a secure home was Alice's trigger. At first she was unable to express her anger in any direct way. Instead, she turned it inward and attempted suicide several times. After months of therapy, she realized that she had a right to be mad. Anger is a normal reaction and should be recognized and confronted and worked through if the person is to regain balance and health.

Alice agonized over the thought that "they had worked so hard for fourteen years to have the all-American dream: new house, comfortable salary, four great kids, and a nice mini-van for the family." But all the material things that were supposed to create happiness didn't protect Alice. Finally, she was able to bring the anger about her loss to the surface and is still working past it. She says that even now she feels mentally unstable and is taking antidepressants. "I just have to take one day at a time."

Responsibility for children may create a major battleground leading to anger and despair. Custody conflicts are common, with the straight spouse declaring that her husband is an unfit parent. Many states do not presently offer statutory protection of the custody rights of homosexual parents, and some judges rule against gays solely because of their sexual orientation. Even when joint custody is allowed, frequently there are angry encounters between the estranged parents. Sandy, for example, reported James to the authorities for child abuse, after their daughter came home bruised after a weekend with her father. It is most unfortunate that the kids are the suffering innocents, caught between their parents in these situations.

Betty, whose children were three and five years old when her husband came out, chafes under his refusal to pay child support, even though her financial need is extreme. The moment of her greatest anger was when Rob admitted that he purposely quit his job to get out of paying child support. Betty's sudden realization that she would be responsible for the two children and all the finances overwhelmed her. "I could've easily strangled him with my bare hands!"

Jealousy preceded anger for Joni. She first learned of David's gay tendencies in an emotional discussion in February. She wasn't convinced at first that her husband was truly gay. She said, "I'll wait a while until he knows for sure. He said he still wasn't certain. He had been feeling these urges for a while and he had to find out." She learned that he had been intimate with three different men and had fallen in love with the one he'd been seeing most recently. When Valentine's Day came, David spent the whole night with his new lover, while Joni sat at home alone. She said, "I never felt so angry and lost! I knew right then, I couldn't wait to leave him. This was killing me!" His betrayal of her and the fact that he waited so long to tell her of his emotional struggles added to her anger and despair.

Disruption of home life, especially where children are involved, creates bitter resentment for some women. Lydia's experience is an example that has already been noted. She left to visit her parents, leaving the children at home with her husband, Jonathan. When she later learned that he had entertained his lover in their bedroom during most of that weekend, she was enraged. She said there were many struggles, some for power, during that time. "Jonathan became authoritarian about everything. There was never any discussion or negotiation possible. He knew the answer right away and that was that. If I disagreed, he would do all he could to undermine the situation. He favored our daughter but was hard on our two sons. Our boys were at-risk. They reacted to get attention and acted out in anti-social behaviors. There were harsh words and defiance. Finally Jonathan had the boys locked up at a mental hospital. After several tests, the doctors found no drugs, no mental problems—just anti-social behavior. Later he sent the boys to a Methodist ranch to work on behavior problems."

Home life was hell for them all. Lydia's absolute low came with a double blow—first, Jonathan told her that his male lover had AIDS and that he had surely been exposed, and then she was fired from her job. These extreme conditions in Lydia's home kindled an abiding resentment and anger that she is only now getting over—more than a decade later.

Health concerns brought on my deepest emotional hole. When he came out to me, Jim assured me that he was safe, but I had to make sure. Within a month after that Memorial Day weekend, when we had our honest talk, my vague worry came to a head. Here is how I described it in my journal. "Lately, the specter of AIDS has worried me. Both of our therapists believe that Jim will continue homosexual encounters, despite his present intention otherwise. They believe it is inevitable. Deb urges me to protect myself and always use condoms. The reality of being at high risk for AIDS is hitting home at last. I don't remember ever using condoms before. The idea is so distasteful to me. It takes six months for the HIV virus antibodies to be detected. While Jim was clean when he last tested in December, he is not necessarily free of HIV now. What sexual experiences has he had since last winter?

"My first AIDS test is set for Tuesday. The whole business is unspeakably embarrassing and nerve-wracking. When Jim returns from Lake Powell, I'll insist that he go for another test too.

"For forty minutes I waited to be called in for my AIDS test at the County Health Department, praying that I'd disappear into the woodwork in the meantime. I sat with my back to the door and buried my face in a book to hide from anyone who might notice me. I kept looking at my left hand, naked without my wedding ring. As I watched the words on the page blur together, I devised and mentally practiced a suitable story: 'I've learned that my lover is bisexual.' I hoped that lie would protect Jim's identity as a gay man.

"Then came the ordeal. A kind young woman led me back to her tiny private office. Businesslike, she started briskly through the printed form's cold questions. She used terms I'd never heard: 'fisting.' (My God! How painful!) I felt like a naïve child. Head bowed in embarrassment, in a meek voice I hardly recognized as my own, I kept asking, 'What does that mean?' Then, 'No! I don't do that!'

"Suddenly, she stopped and took a long moment to study my face. I shrank under her gaze as she began to realize my anguish. It appears that I don't do most sexual acts. Am I a dolt, a Victorian child—or just lucky not to know about these things?

"I couldn't lie after all. I told the caseworker the truth: 'I'm married to a gay man and I'm here at my therapist's insistence and out of my own fear.' She asked if I had used my real name when I filled out the paperwork. I had. She gave me a blank form and advised me to make up a name to protect my identity and my husband. I wrote 'Karen Green' on the fresh form and watched as she tore up my original paperwork and threw it into the wastebasket under her desk.

"After that, her manner became even gentler. Her face and voice softened. She seemed apologetic as she hurried through her litany of personal questions and drew blood for the test. She showed me how to protect myself with condoms, recited the necessary precautions, and sent me on my way with a bright pink cloth packet of condoms, lubricant, and a ridiculous flip cartoon book showing a penis rising, then slipping a condom raincoat on.

"My face was flushed and my eyes full of tears as I sank into the driver's seat of my car and tried to pull myself together. I sat in the health department parking lot for several minutes, feeling completely drained. That day undoubtedly marked the greatest humiliation of my life."

I'll never forget the vivid pain I felt that day. That single experience brought out my worst hours of resentment and despair and left a permanent emotional scar—the reminder of all I had lost.

Dangers of "The Black Hole"

There are as many triggers for anger as there are individuals in mixed orientation marriages, as these diverse examples show. But the greatest danger of this stage is getting stuck in this emotional trap. The most unhappy woman I encountered was also the most angry. It was odd—she was studying at a nearby school of theology, preparing for the Christian ministry, yet her conversation about her gay husband overflowed with venom. She spouted her hatred and disdain for him and for all men like him. During one meeting with several other straight spouses, she dominated the conversation all evening with her emotional barrage. It was exhausting just to watch. I came away wondering how she could ever work as a spiritual healer when her own soul seemed so wounded and sick. This was apparently not a passing phase either since she had been going through the same list of complaints for months, fueling her own fury.

There are other notable pitfalls as well. Homophobia is common—stereotypical thinking that demeans all homosexuals and turns into hatred for them. Illness is another obvious result. Sandy had a terrible cough, with laryngitis and flu-like symptoms, for many months. The doctors couldn't find a cause. She's now convinced that it was a psychosomatic result of her deep-seated resentment and anger over James' deception. Violence toward a gay husband or his lover is also a real possibility, as well as a whole variety of self-destructive behavior. Alice's suicide attempts and Katie's alcohol abuse are examples.

It is obvious that the emotions of this stage are terribly complex and confusing. Most women I interviewed had a difficult time separating their anger from their sense of utter despair. The two states are usually intertwined, each feeding the other, making them even more debilitating. Some wives spoke of life losing its value. Suicidal thoughts were frequent. Alice said, "Why keep living when everything is lost." Trust and security are gone. All aspects of life are called into question. One grieves as for a death.

When Jim's mother learned that I planned to write a book, she wondered what its title would be. Before I could answer, she suggested *Death After Life*. Indeed, this *is* the death of the past, made more fearful by an uncertain future. The black hole is surely the lowest point of all in a straight spouse's journey.

Is there any hope? Will this horrible ordeal ever end? For most women who have walked this path, the answer is yes. Their predictable, necessary period of anger is the darkest night before the dawning light of recovery. The worst is past because the woman's very anger is a signal that she has turned the corner and has begun to think of her own needs. She can then open to new possibilities and take responsibility for her own well-being. So the arduous process of digging out of the black hole of anger and despair often brings clearer vision to see a better future.

6

An Action Guide to Wholeness

The purpose of this book is to demonstrate to straight women that they are not alone in the challenges of a mixed orientation marriage. Others have walked this path with no less frustration and fear and we have survived. Some enjoy an even better life afterward. You can too!

The chapters so far have focused on various facets of our journey into our gay husbands' closet of secrecy. Most of the women I interviewed consider their experience as the single most significant event in their lives. Whether our marriages ended or remained intact, we all faced hard choices and went through recognizable, progressive steps to work through the challenges of the situation. Individual stories demonstrate many similarities in ways of coping. Every woman who contributed information for this book offers her experience as a piece of the road map for those who follow.

By studying these women's positive actions—the things that worked—it is possible to draw some useful advice to pass on to those who are just beginning this arduous process. After a trauma of this magnitude, healing is needed for the whole person. Raw emotions beg for compassion and loving kindness; confusion demands understanding. Individuals differ markedly in the amount of time it takes to heal the wounds of a gay-straight marriage, and some never completely recover, but for those who do, this remarkable event becomes a catalyst for surprising growth.

A proactive, intentional approach is definitely needed for success. Full recovery is nearly impossible without outside help, professional counseling, broadening of viewpoint, and positive personal action. This chapter and the next may therefore be the most important in the book, because they explore some of the activities and resources and attitudes that have helped others recover their wholeness. Focusing on mind, body, emotions, and spirit, this information is offered as a straight spouse survival manual—practical advice and inspiring examples that suggest ways to heal and open the next chapter of her life.

Mind

Sexual Orientation: Basic Facts

When Bonnie discovered her husband's bisexuality through a letter he had written to a gay friend, she said that she felt very unlearned. She knew absolutely nothing about homosexual behavior or homophobia or anything related. Carlotta was similarly uneducated about the subject—as were most of the women I interviewed. These two women methodically studied and learned the facts about sexual orientation, thus avoiding much of the intolerance born of ignorance. Their work paid dividends: they are two of the best success stories in this book, both leading happy, productive, and rewarding lives today. Their example is worth following. A few basic facts are offered here as a foundation for further exploration, and a resource list of recommended readings may be found in the appendix.

The American Psychological Association defines four components of sexuality. They are:

- Biological Sex—the gender of the physical body
- Gender Identity—the psychological sense of being male or female
- Social Sex Role—adherence to cultural norms for feminine and masculine behavior
- Sexual Orientation—an enduring emotional, romantic, sexual, or physical attraction to individuals of a particular gender.

Sexual orientation involves self-concept and how we understand and feel about our deepest individuality—who we are in our own minds. As an internal concept, our orientation therefore differs from our sexual behavior, (i.e., how we act out this self-concept).

Professionals agree that sexual orientation is not a choice. It is an innate characteristic that emerges, usually in early adolescence, without any prior sexual experience. It is not taught nor learned; it is not "caught"; it cannot be "recruited." It is the natural and normal way of being for homosexual individuals. While scientists don't fully understand how a particular orientation develops, there are various, well-known theories about its source. Genetic or inborn hormonal factors are most often cited, along with life experiences during childhood. Most professionals believe that sexual orientation emerges through complex interactions of biological, psychological, and social factors.

Moreover, there are varying degrees of homosexual orientation, and the way sexuality is acted out may change over time. The Kinsey Scale is often cited to illustrate the degrees between zero, exclusively heterosexual, and six, exclusively homosexual. While only 4 percent of the men studied regarded themselves as exclusively gay, 57 percent reported homosexual encounters leading to orgasm sometime in their post-adolescent years. Half of the men studied revealed that they had experienced homoerotic attractions. An individual's sexual orientation thus may fall anywhere on a wide spectrum between the extremes of heterosexuality and homosexuality.

Today, the consensus among mental health professionals is that homosexuality is neither an emotional disorder nor a mental illness. In 1973, as a result of years of research in the field, the American Psychiatric Association confirmed this view by removing the term "homosexuality" from the official manual of mental and emotional disorders. Two years later, the American Psychological Association passed a resolution confirming their support of that action. Research by both organizations has reaffirmed the position that homosexuality is not an illness. It therefore does not need to be "fixed" or "cured."

Another point of professional agreement is that, while sexual orientation may be disguised (not acted upon), it cannot be changed. A few therapists and religious groups continue to try changing individuals' sexual orientation, but the results disappoint them. The American Psychological Association reports that their scrutiny of reports of "successful conversion" invites skepticism. Most of these efforts are made by organizations with a negative ideological bias, rather than by scientific researchers. Their treatments and outcomes are poorly documented and the follow-up time after treatment is too short to claim real change. In 1998 The American Psychiatric Association declared that reparative therapy to change a person's sexual orientation is ineffective and potentially dangerous. While sexual behavior may change for a period of time, sexual orientation remains the same.

In 1990 the American Psychological Association stated its position clearly. Even if it were possible, changing sexual orientation would require a complete reversal of self-concept, social identity, emotions, and romantic sensibility. It would disrupt the person's entire sense of self, requiring a radical psychological intervention, which would raise deep ethical questions. Even if the gay or lesbian person earnestly desired this change, it could not be accomplished. In short, scientific evidence indicates that efforts to convert sexual orientation from homosexual to heterosexual are not successful, and attempts to make such conversions do great psychological harm. Sexual orientation cannot be voluntarily or forcefully changed. Understanding these basic facts helps us avoid some popular myths that are rooted in heterosexism (giving priority status and value to heterosexuality), or homophobia (the irrational fear of homosexuality or homosexual persons).

Recognizing Homophobia

Homophobia was first defined as a true phobia in the early 1970s by Dr. George Weinberg. Because they experience mild to acute fear, homophobes dehumanize homosexuals, judging the whole person on the exclusive basis of sexual orientation. Depending upon the intensity of their fear, homophobic actions may range from mere avoidance to active violence against gays.

Homophobia is an imminent probability for any straight spouse for obvious reasons. For these particular women, it has an experiential function, helping them make sense of their feelings about their mixed orientation marriages. Their fear is based on a felt need to protect themselves from further harm. However, while gay bashing may appear to be a way of getting revenge for our own wounds, it has a decidedly detrimental long-term effect. It feeds anger and intolerance and hatred, which only turn inward to create more personal pain. Hatred hurts the hater, not the hated. So becoming aware of and eliminating homophobic attitudes is an important step toward recovery and future happiness.

What are the signs of homophobia? How do we know if we have it? Some common symptoms are attitudinal markers.

- Acute awareness of people in public places who exhibit gay stereotypes. The belief that you can spot homosexuals simply by their appearance or mannerisms.

- Physical avoidance of people you assume to be gay. Assuming that any casual touch has sexual overtones.

- Joking about or deriding gays through derogatory, stereotyping terms.

- Experiencing revulsion when witnessing public affection between homosexual lovers.

- Feeling repulsed by gay rights demonstrations.

- Patronizing gay people; feeling superior to them.

- Reluctance to find and study factual information about homosexuality and sexual orientation.

While this list is only a small sampling, it suggests the foundation of homophobia. Heterosexism looks only at the trait of sexuality, not at the complexity of the whole person. Thus, any myopic attitude or action that implies that a gay person is merely a sexual being, not a complete, unique individual, can be recognized as homophobic.

Mental health and medical authorities have identified other facts that dispel popular heterosexist myths. Here are some major ones.

- Homosexuality is not a rare occurrence. PFLAG estimates that one of every four families has a gay member and about 10 percent of the world's population is homosexual.

- Gays and lesbians come from every race, religion, ethnic background, culture, socio-economic level, and every country of the world.

- There is no uniform "gay community." Individuals exhibit all the variety of interests and activities found among heterosexual people.

- Stereotyped caricatures of gays are fallacious. Gay people and heterosexuals enjoy the same ordinary pursuits of daily living. Both groups may engage in stable, long-lasting relationships, hold responsible jobs, seek conventional entertainment, travel to the same places, vote, shop, and pay taxes. The only common factor that identifies them as gay is their sexual orientation.

- While some gays do fit popular stereotypes of homosexuality, most do not. They are more likely to look and act exactly the same way as heterosexual people. Attempts to identify gays merely by appearance are therefore often unsuccessful.

- Homosexual people are rarely involved in child abuse. Ninety percent of child molestation, sexual attack, and child battering are committed by heterosexual men, according to the U.S. Department of Health, Education, and Welfare. The molesters are usually family members or people known by the family.

- Most transvestites are heterosexual males. Cross-dressing is not necessarily an expression of homosexuality.

For a straight spouse, making a commitment to learn the facts about sexual orientation is a giant step forward. Understanding your gay mate's motivation and needs should encourage actions and attitudes that help to heal wounds for both husband and wife. For additional information on relevant subjects, please refer to the resources listed in the appendix. The Web site list is particularly helpful for current research on specific areas of interest. Dispelling negative myths about sexual orientation is an essential step toward emotional recovery.

Body

Nearly every woman I interviewed experienced some sort of illness after her husband's disclosure. Beth's laryngitis, Bonnie's bleeding ulcers, and Sandy's persistent cough are good examples. Emotions and health are intrinsically connected, so any intense shock increases the probability of sickness.

Simply having a gay partner is inherently risky, assuming that the husband is acting on his homosexual impulses. The discussion in chapter four indicated some of the health risks that must be considered. At the very least, AIDS tests are imperative, repeated every six months, along with safe sex practices for those who continue intimacy with their gay spouse.

Beyond that obvious requirement, it is also useful to have a thorough physical examination and to pay particular attention to health-inducing, preventive measures, such as a wholesome diet, sufficient sleep, and regular exercise. Though this sounds obvious, a great conscious effort to take care of ourselves is imperative when we are depressed and upset. But the return of a greater sense of well-being is worth the effort.

Fueling the body with nourishing food is a good first step. Consciously choosing natural, whole, fresh, organic foods makes a huge difference in how well we feel. Learn about good nutrition. Read package labels. Replace overprocessed, fatty, sugary junk food with well-balanced, regular meals featuring nutritious fresh vegetables, fruits, and whole grains. If weight gain or loss is a problem, these more healthful whole foods help the body regain its natural balance and energy.

Many doctors recommend vitamin and mineral supplements to ensure the intake of sufficient nutrients. Check your own doctor's advice on type and amount of supplements, since overdosing can also be harmful. Just be conscious of everything you are consuming and take the time to plan meals that will build health. These daily choices actually enhance self-worth: "I eat well because I'm worth it." That is powerful self-talk!

Sleeplessness is a real problem for people in the midst of grief or crisis. Virtually all the women I talked with had trouble sleeping. Most talked of waking at 2:00 or 3:00 A.M. and staying awake for hours, then falling asleep shortly before they had to get up in the morning. Fatigue added to everything else they were enduring. Under such circumstances, it is easy to fall into the habit of using sleeping pills, either over-the-counter or prescription sedatives. Alcohol abuse is a real possibility as well. A sad, exhausted person will do almost anything to get some sleep. These chemical substances may offer a short-term solution, but actually make insomnia worse. In addition, they carry the greater danger of dependence or even addiction. Moreover, drugs and alcohol exacerbate the typical depression the women are already experiencing.

There are better ways to deal with insomnia and its resulting exhaustion. Simply breathing deeply can help the body to relax. Imagine the in-breath coming up through the fingertips and up the arms, and the slow out-breath moving down through the midsection and legs and out the toes. Keep the shoulders relaxed during deep breathing and feel the whole body relax.

One woman suggested a progressive relaxation technique that helped her relax within about five minutes. Starting with the muscles of one hand, make a fist. Hold the fist tightly for about seven seconds, then relax it completely and feel the difference between tight and relaxed muscles. Tighten and hold, then relax major muscle groups in sequence, moving from the feet and legs, to the abdomen, then the hips, the upper back, then both arms, then the shoulders (bring them up to the ears), then the neck. Tighten and inhale, then release and exhale.

Holding mental images that are associated with feelings of peace, safety, and contentment also help during these breathing exercises. It might be a scene of natural beauty, like a mountain stream, or a happy childhood place—any memory that comforts you. My most helpful images were drawn from pure imagination. I had collected several small models of old English cottages. My particular favorite was the Sussex Cottage by David Winter. It is a small stone house with a red tile roof with a single dormer window—probably a loft bedroom. When I was sleepless and disturbed, I went to "my cottage." In my mind, I walked up the cobblestone path, through the door of that cottage, and explored every part of the house. I imagined a living room with a fireplace and well-filled bookshelves, a comfortable easy chair, and a desk under a window overlooking woods in the back. I "saw" the dark wood floors, shining under a Persian rug. I imagined myself walking up the stairs to the bedroom and back down to the kitchen and dining room. Each of the four rooms was entirely furnished in my mind. Whenever I lay awake at night, I visited my English cottage and rested there. These familiar mental pictures usually took me out of my current worries and made me feel safe and quiet enough to sleep.

Other practical ways to aid natural sleep are well-known. Avoid caffeine particularly late in the day. Eat light fare at an early dinner hour, reserving heavier or spicier foods for lunch. Avoid excessive alcohol. Develop personal rituals that signal bedtime. Light reading with a cup of hot herbal tea helped me. I stopped watching the late news, rife with incessant violence and disturbing images. Instead, I enjoyed the quiet of the night or listened to some favorite music after a relaxing warm shower. Several women recommended long, luxurious bubble baths during acute periods of grief. Research also suggests that assuming the same particular posture when going to bed may help induce sleep. In short, whatever brings comfort, warmth, relaxation, and quiet may encourage healing sleep.

Body work of some sort is also an excellent emotional support. My therapist prescribed regular massage during the months I was adjusting to Jim's truth. I was storing all my tension in my neck and shoulders and experienced daily stress-related headaches at the time. The gentle massage and acupressure helped relieve my pain. I also discovered that massage helped me open up to my own sadness and to express it more freely. I was able to weep unashamedly on the massage table—a healthy reaction for one who had learned too well to suppress emotion. I became close friends with Jill, my massage therapist, and always felt refreshed both physically and emotionally after a treatment.

Exercise may be the most important key of all. Physical exercise is a huge aid to restful sleep and a great way to work off tension and depression. Whether you choose walking, biking, swimming, or any other sport, physical activity lifts the spirits. Gardening was my best outlet. Not only was it strenuous labor, I also had the pleasure of seeing the beautiful results of my work. Joining a fitness class at the YMCA helped me stay strong during the winter months. Working out with weights and circuit training with various exercise machines enhanced strength, endurance, and my general sense of well-being. It also introduced me to a whole new set of friends at a time when I felt isolated. Of course, a formal class is certainly not required, but some sort of physical activity done with intention is beneficial—taking the stairs instead of the elevator, parking the car at the far side of the parking lot, even doing ordinary household chores with directed energy. The point is to keep moving, keep physically active.

While these suggestions for strengthening the body may seem obvious, they are difficult to remember during the depth of crisis. But after a straight wife asks her turning-point question—"What about me?"— it becomes possible to honor her own worth and work toward greater physical health. Caring for ourselves with clear intention is another way of saying, "I am a valuable and important person and I deserve to be strong and well."

Emotions

Confronting the Isolation

A wife's sense of isolation is perhaps the most painful part of being in the closet in a mixed orientation marriage. Intense loneliness seems inevitable. Most of the women I talked with felt that they were the only people in the world who had ever known this struggle. When I faced the fact that Jim is gay and that I had to keep everything secret, I was sure that no one else had ever felt that lonely pain. I felt completely abandoned and alone. My emotional stress was indescribable.

But I was lucky. From the beginning, I was fortunate to have one outlet for the pressure: my counselor, Deb. I believe that I would have imploded without her help and am convinced that professional therapy was essential for me. Other women in this book who sought such help enthusiastically recommended it; those who carried the burden alone had a much harder time. Some waited for years to talk through their experience, painfully delaying their eventual recovery. Every one of those women strongly urged others to get help fast.

In searching for an appropriate counselor, keep in mind that not all professionals have experience with mixed orientation couples. Shop carefully for one who is knowledgeable, open, empathetic, and realistic in expectations. Ask about their specific type of experience and have a trial session before committing to long-term work. Make sure your personalities are compatible so that trust can be built. Feeling confident and comfortable with your therapist is the foundation for counseling success.

In addition to finding a competent counselor either privately or with government or non-profit assistance, it is also most helpful to confide in someone who knows and cares for you—perhaps a trusted friend or close relative. Several women mentioned that their sisters were their strongest support. In my case, it was necessary for a long time to shield the whole family from the truth. I got lonelier and lonelier as weeks passed. Then, without prior planning, I impulsively poured out my sorrow to two different friends. Both were absolutely trustworthy and able to keep the confidence. I felt tremendous relief. As time passed, I didn't talk about it often with either of them, but I felt their strong, quiet support. Just knowing that they were standing by, I didn't feel so alone.

Furry friends also count! Many of the women I talked with spoke of the comfort they received from their pets, and I certainly felt supported by the unconditional acceptance of my cat, Sundance. Stroking her soft fur and hearing her calm purr, I poured out my pent-up affection. That soft back also caught a lot of tears. I wrote in my journal, "Little Sundance is the dearest friend I have right now. Staying close by, her steady green eyes studying my face, she seems to understand the recurring sadness in this house, quietly sharing it. Her gray striped coat is silky and comforting against my cheek. With Jim often emotionally absent, it helps to have a warm, living creature to touch and love. More important, she returns my love. I felt an electric moment of recognition this morning when I read something by Jean Cocteau: 'I love cats because I enjoy my home; and, little by little, they become its visible soul.' I cling now to Sundance and my home."

Besides a counselor or close relative or friend, there are other resources for women in the closet. One organization, The Straight Spouse Network (SSN), is focused specifically on our invisible minority. A major purpose is to provide a safe setting for straight spouses to meet and confide in each other. Only women who have direct experience with this issue can fully understand the realities and nuances of this journey. Talking freely about one's secret anguish to others who have first-hand knowledge is tremendously healing. Regular group meetings allow women to network confidentially with peers, build important friendships, and provide outreach for others who are new to the sisterhood. Supportive discussions help women to ground themselves again and to rebuild their confidence. Most important, attendance at these meetings demonstrates clearly that one is not alone.

The SSN provides personal encouragement and accurate information through 35 United States chapters, with spouse contacts in nearly every state and seven foreign countries. The organization also offers an array of Internet support groups. An established, respected organization, it serves straight spouses, other family members, professionals, and community organizations. It may offer referrals for low cost HIV testing and information on AIDS. Membership in SSN specifically includes the heterosexual spouses and partners, current or former, of gay, lesbian, bisexual, or transgender mates. Its mission for all members is to reach out, heal, and build bridges. For information about SSN, call 510-525-0200, or write 8215 Terrace Drive, El Cerrito, CA 94530-3058. The Web site www.ssnetwk.org offers current information and contact data.

Now an independent organization, SSN began in 1986 as a task force established by Parents, Families and Friends of Lesbians and Gays (PFLAG), which has over 400 affiliates across the United States and in eleven other countries. Founded in 1981, PFLAG is a family-based organization that addresses the broader educational issues of the entire homosexual sector, advocating respect for diversity and justice for gay people. Literature, newsletters, resource lists, tapes, and videos encourage and educate members on health and human rights issues. Some chapters have telephone help-lines to answer questions and aid networking. Group meetings provide dialogue about sexual orientation and offer emotional support for gays, lesbians and bisexuals and their parents, relatives, and friends.

Like the SSN, PFLAG is a tax-exempt, non-profit organization, not affiliated with any political or religious institution. For more information about PFLAG, call the organization headquarters at 202-467-8180, or write 1726 M Street NW, Suite 400, Washington, DC 20036. The PFLAG Web site at www.pflag.org also offers current information and reading material to purchase or download on your computer.

If these particular support groups are not available in your city, call your nearest state, county, or city AIDS Project to contact local organizations and to ask for referral service. Consult the yellow pages under "AIDS Information" for phone numbers in your area. The local county health department may also have referral information and printed materials on related subjects.

Why are SSN and other support groups so valuable? Obviously association with other spouses in the same fix dispels the myth that "I'm the only one." Hearing other stories also helps count their own blessings. It is harder to feel sorry for yourself when you hear women in the same room report stories that are worse than yours.

A well-known Buddhist teaching illustrates the point. It is the story of Indra's Net. The image is that the universe is a net of infinite proportions. At every connection of the net, there is a highly reflective jewel. Each jewel reflects all the others, like a mirror, or a crystal. Each jewel also reflects all the *reflected* images, repeating the light again and again. To see one point of light is to see all the others. These lights go on into infinity. The lesson of Indra's Net is that no light is separate from others. All is one. One is all. When a wounded wife connects with others in the same pain, they share their light and their understanding. They know that they are not alone.

Strengthening Family Relationships

When a gay husband comes out, everyone involved is thrown into emotional turmoil. One of the most difficult challenges is helping the whole family understand and accept this new reality. The task is complicated if children are involved, regardless of their age. It is common for American families to deny suffering in their homes. American parents try to shield children from pain, thereby substituting a great silence. If anything is said at all, it is repackaged to mask its seriousness. This is the wrong approach. Denial and pretense inflict greater pain than truth. Both children and adults must eventually learn the truth—that suffering is part of the human condition. There are partings and losses, as well as happiness and successes. Experts agree that children should be told about their father's homosexuality, with the proviso that the information be provided skillfully at their level of understanding. Moreover, it is far better for them to hear the news directly from their own parents, not from outsiders.

Generally speaking, young children need direct, repeated assurance of love from both parents. PFLAG suggests a simple statement like "Mommy and Daddy still love each other and you, but Daddy loves someone else now, too." Small children cannot comprehend detailed information about sexuality or homosexuality, but they do understand what love is and they can see it demonstrated through caring actions. Lee, for example, said that her daughter was young at the time and didn't really understand—"She knew simply that we were separating and that she would end up with two bedrooms. Now that the child is seven, she still doesn't fully understand, but she has a foundation for the details that will come when she's older. She has been with her dad when he was with a man, and they put their arms around each other. She commented on it, and Randy asked her if it was okay, and she said yes. I think I would have done the same thing if this had been an ordinary divorce situation. I think it really helped that we did not fight, and that we did get along as well as we did. I think the big thing is not to fight or argue, to be adult and handle the situation in a mature manner."

It is important to be honest, but try to reduce the information to really simple terms that the child can understand: "Mommy loves men, and Daddy loves men, too." It may help to use tangible props, like Barbie and Ken dolls, to talk about it. Books on homosexuality as a family issue are also available, some written for children in specific age ranges. Check with your local librarian for help in finding suitable printed materials.

School-age children can grasp more detailed information. At some intuitive level, they may already know. It is important to bridge the gap between what these older children feel and what they have been told in the past. They need to learn to trust their own feelings and at the same time trust what their parents tell them. Building this ongoing trust is essential if the family ties are to remain strong through and beyond this challenge.

Older children's grasp of homosexuality will likely be complicated by the homophobic attitudes of their acquaintances. It is important to reinforce the fact that homosexuality and heterosexuality are both part of the broad spectrum of sexual orientation. Open communication is essential, providing accurate information and answers to questions. Resentment over the change in family life may surface, calling for extra emotional support and patient understanding. Both parents need to offer the security of their love during months or even years of transition.

Teenagers may be especially vulnerable. Above all, adolescents fear being different. They may therefore be particularly susceptible to anti-gay attitudes, since homophobia is especially intense among adolescents. Teens may also react to fears based in their own sexual confusion at this volatile age, particularly if they previously suspected their father's homosexuality. (They are usually more aware than the parents realize. For example, Susan's older children intuitively knew, long before she did.) Anger, withdrawal, and lowered self-esteem are common at best in the teen years. During this crisis, the potential of substance abuse or other self-destructive behavior is imminent.

On the other hand, having mixed orientation parents may present unforeseen opportunities. If the situation is handled skillfully, the whole family may improve interpersonal communication and increase their tolerance for diversity. I interviewed Maria, daughter of Carlotta and Daniel, whose story has surfaced throughout this book. She and her older brother learned about their father's orientation four years before they could talk about it outside their home. They were both protecting their father's career as a school superintendent. This mature eighteen year-old praised both her parents for their complete honesty. "It was the most important thing to me. Nothing was hidden from me. I could ask anything!" Above all, teenagers need accurate, complete information and honest answers to all their questions.

Maria brought out another important point, the necessity of humor in maintaining balance. "You either laugh or cry when you go through this. We told gay jokes at the dinner table and laughed together." Because of their necessity to stay together as a group in the closet for such a long time, they turned to each other for support, and it brought the family close. Though Carlotta and Daniel did get divorced, Maria and her brother are still close to their father and his new partner, as well as to their mother. Maria believes their prolonged process was useful. Her best advice? "Take it really slow. For us, it wasn't traumatic because we had time to work through each stage together."

What if your children are on their own, out of the nest? Even grown children need special help as they adjust to the discovery of a gay parent. Again, complete openness is recommended. Don't deny your pain! Instead, try to discover through honesty your heart's capacity to bear great pain. Relate to the truth of the situation. Jim and I chose to speak to each of our sons and other close family members together and in person. We all supported each other emotionally through the initial shock, and, like Carlotta and Daniel, we promised that we would always be family, despite the changes that Jim's disclosure would surely bring. We were determined not to denigrate each other or the truth of the situation, and we were rewarded by our sons' response of unconditional love.

Since most mixed orientation couples eventually divorce, as Jim and I did, the family break-up adds to the pain of the children, whatever their age. They may experience feelings of abandonment, insecurity, and conflicts of loyalty. While there is no magic formula to help young people through this experience, open communication and frequent reassurance of love from both parents help. I asked the women I interviewed to give their best advice on helping children work through this crisis. They agreed on several major points:

1. Think and plan before you speak. Plan carefully what to say and how to say it. It may be better to give children blocks of information in sequence, allowing time for them to adjust at each stage. For example, Carlotta and Daniel first told their teenagers the fact that Daniel is gay. Later, they talked at length about their ongoing loyalty to each other and their determination to remain connected to each other as family, no matter how that worked out. Finally, they told the youngsters of their decision to divorce, reassuring them that their family's love was intact. Months passed between each of these conversations, allowing everyone involved to process the meaning of each stage. Carlotta believes it helped her kids, aged twelve and sixteen then, to have lots of time between these plateaus to ask questions, absorb the implications, and generally get used to each separate idea.

2. Be honest. As soon as possible, tell the truth to the whole family, preferably face to face. Secrecy damages relationships.

3. Educate yourself and convey information accurately. Use the resources from the appendix and other sources to get the facts on sexual orientation and related matters. Research the issues and teach your children what they need to know.

4. Don't spread your own hang-ups. Sandy urged women to convey the situation as "the way it is." Difficult as it is, try not to color communication with your own anger or judgment. State facts as honestly and clearly as possible, free of homophobic bias.

5. Don't seek children as allies. One of the most destructive practices is to encourage divided loyalties. It is tempting to recruit children as allies against the offending spouse. Don't! Turning children against their father hurts everyone involved. Moreover, when the young people realize that they were used as emotional

pawns in this way, they will turn against the manipulative parent with a vengeance.

6. Engage professional help, if needed. A straight spouse has enough challenge in coping with her own loss and pain. Add to that the needs of her children, and she may be overwhelmed. Counseling for both the wife and the children may be helpful.

Clearly, when possible, it is to everyone's advantage to protect family relationships in the long term. This is one important piece of a larger issue, regaining emotional balance.

Finding Balance Again

Every woman I spoke with talked about her emotional roller coaster. When Jim and I were still in the closet, I wrote of my own uncertainty. "As our car crawled through the rolling wheat lands of western Oklahoma, doubts crept out of the darkness of my mind. Am I being an utter fool? The big question is whether I can handle all this knowledge without jealousy or self-deprecation. I've agreed that Jim can go out, as long as he doesn't lie to me. I know that harnessing primordial drives is unrealistic and he's convinced me that homosexual celibacy isn't workable. But what will this do to my own self-esteem? Can I meet my own sexual needs? Can I carry his heavy secret successfully? Am I too broad-minded? Should I just give up on this weird marriage and build a new life alone or with another man? The only way to answer these questions is day, by day, by day, by day. Live it out in the moment and experiment."

At this time I was doing my best to put myself in Jim's place and to understand his needs and motivations, drives, and fears. Because of the value we both placed on our relationship, we tested our endurance against the "normal" mores of the world. We did have good weapons in that battle—mutual love, desire to succeed, three decades of history together, the respect of our traditional families (in their ignorance of our reality), liberal friends, regard in the community, competent counselors, and, most important, evolving spirituality. Each of us tried to put ourselves in the other's place. Indeed, after more than thirty years of marriage, it was hard to separate our "selves." In retrospect, all this made our path easier.

But in the end, it didn't work. We did have prejudice and fear and latent anger. We did have basic needs that the other could not meet. But we consistently refused to attack each other. When one or the other would fall into the black hole, we tried to understand. Perhaps most of all, we began to learn patience. Like Carlotta and Daniel, our professional lives required a long, four-year process toward eventual divorce. Everything we experienced was a teacher. Every lesson was fuel for waking up to our new reality. Step by step, we were moving toward new and separate lives.

Other wives spoke of similar experience. As they worked through their emotional upheavals, they spoke of several specific actions that were beneficial.

1. Rely on trusted friends. The importance of close friends cannot be overstressed. Talk about your pain. Avoid the tendency to withdraw completely into the loneliness of your own mind.

2. Reach out to the larger community. Get out! Foster new friendships, walk in the park, catch an art show, join a hiking club, exercise at the Y. If you don't have company, go alone. Find some reason to change your routine and meet some new people. It is so easy to become reclusive and curl up into yourself. Resist that pull and face the public.

3. Cultivate new friends. The women who separated from their husbands right away found themselves sitting at home alone. Most of their network was among couple friends. While they were still close to those people, they were only half a couple. It is lonely at first. Annie and Lee both found new male friends through a dating service. They highly recommended it, since the men they previously knew were already married. Properly selected, there are good organizations that help single people meet each other. It is also possible to build a new romantic relationship on the basis of an existing friendship. Many mature single people gravitate to their oldest, now dearest, friends!

4. Develop new interests. After separation, there is often more time for self-development. There is also pent-up emotion that needs a positive outlet. This is the time to enroll in a continuing education class, take up a new hobby, join a sports club, or explore art in a new way. I learned Ikebana—Japanese flower arranging—and took another class to explore several traditional Eastern arts: Yoga, Tai chi, Aikido and Kyudo. It took me out of my smaller self and into a wider world of mind-body awareness. What we "know" from past experience is only a miniscule slice of all that we do not know. Now is the time to explore!

5. Look toward the future. What's next? Achieving emotional balance is tied directly to this question. Are you ready to live with your choice of remaining married? Are you ready to meet the challenge of living on your own? What is your course of action here? If you are already engaged in a satisfying (or acceptable) career/job, that will be a stabilizing factor. If not—how can you prepare for the next step? Security in work is an essential component of emotional balance. If the next step requires "retooling" with new job skills, then go for it! Several of the women I talked

with were returning to school to be ready for their new lives—renewing nursing certificates, working on a master's or a ministerial degree. One developed a new career path in working with hospice patients. The point is to plan ahead for a satisfying future.

Meeting the emotional challenge of a mixed orientation marriage is the hardest part for most straight spouses. But our emotions are rooted in the most important ground of all—the spirit.

Spirit

Reconcile Religious Issues

"Deep in their roots, all flowers keep the light," wrote poet Theodore Roethke. That light of personal spiritual insight can best illumine the darkness of discovery of a mixed orientation marriage. These circumstances call upon our deepest reserves of spiritual practice—whether it comes from a traditional religion or our own philosophical path. Here is perhaps the most important resource for renewal.

Rather than offering peace, however, many religious organizations add to a straight wife's anguish because of their conflict over sexual orientation. Homosexuality is still a controversial subject in many traditional religions. Christian denominations all base their beliefs on the Bible, but their interpretation of biblical meaning varies tremendously. The major dividing line between these groups is how they understand homosexual behavior. If they believe sexual orientation is a *choice*, they regard homosexuality as a sin; if they believe sexual orientation is *innate*, determined at creation, they are more likely to accept it as part of the normal spectrum. Conflicting simplistic answers, supported by proof-texts from the Scriptures, abound. The controversy rages between and within sects and denominations. The resulting confusion makes things even harder for a straight spouse.

PFLAG addressed this controversy by surveying authoritative sources from three Jewish groups and nine Christian denominations. They hoped to learn how religious experts viewed homosexuality. The complete results of their survey appear in their booklet, "Is Homosexuality a Sin?" Most of the religious leaders surveyed agreed on three points:

- "God does not regard homosexuality as a sin."

- "The Scriptures were written before the word homosexual existed. Where there is objection to same-gender sexual expression, it is because those actions were exploitative and oppressive, rather than loving and caring. The writers and interpreters of the Bible were influenced by the social, cultural, and moral attitudes of their time, and limited by the scientific knowledge then available."

- "God approves of gays pledging their love, provided each does so in a constructive, loving, non-selfish way and shows respect for the other's rights and dignity."

Truth may be absolute, but our concept of it grows and changes. It is important for every straight spouse to examine her belief structure and draw comfort from it while she heals her private wounds. This may require modification of previous assumptions or even changing from one spiritual community to another, but the resulting growth is liberating. During the time I was exploring the meaning of Jim's coming out, I spent months studying Eastern philosophical thought. For me, it provided a spiritual ground that sustained me through all my changes. Becoming a Buddhist was the outer manifestation of a whole paradigm shift for me. I honestly believe that shift saved my life, or at least my sanity. Other women in this book found different answers. All are valid; all fit their unique needs. The important point is to seek and find reconciliation with some belief structure that will serve *you* as steady ground in a shifting world.

Find Your Own Path

The women in this book who adjusted most readily to their mixed orientation marriage—or its demise—had some method of feeding themselves spiritually. There were many variations, but each individual found succor in her chosen practice. The examples that follow are just that. They are not prescriptions. They do, however, illustrate some of the ways women have addressed their deepest inner needs.

Bonnie relied on her lifelong Christian faith to carry her through her transition. She said, "It's amazing what you can stand up to in life when you fall on your knees in prayer." A couple's group that met regularly at their church supported both Bonnie and her husband emotionally during several years after he told her his secret. They met with the group during all the time she and her former husband continued their marriage. After their eventual separation she found a new church home when she relocated to another state. "Sometimes faith was on top or sometimes undergirding, but it was always in the mixture. It was always surrounding."

While Bonnie never wavered in her church association, others fell away from the religion of their childhood, then rediscovered their faith during crisis. Sylvia, for example, renewed her faith after fifteen years of not attending mass. "My turning point toward recovery was when I went to Poland and walked 165 miles in nine days—a pilgrimage—in my homeland. In Czestochowa,

I saw the Black Madonna, an icon for my Catholic faith, and wept profusely before her image. I knew then I was on my way to being healed."

Not all spiritual healing occurs in the setting of organized religion. Katie has aided her own spiritual healing through helping others, though she insists that healing is endless and ongoing. "I feel as if I'm in constant recovery. My ex-husband continues to be the catalyst that propels me to deeper levels of healing—from sexual abuse, from lack of self-esteem, from shame. It's been a process, and every step has come at the perfect time, it seems."

Katie has a sense of vocation, a calling to work with the dying. "Few are called to do the work of many," she says. She is brought in by hospice to be with people in their very last days, staying present with the patient until death comes. She finds contentment in her important work and has devoted herself to it. "To facilitate my work, I have simplified everything in my life, having the barest of essentials in terms of home, possessions, and even relationships. I live a life of monastic discipline in order to maintain the physical, emotional, and spiritual fitness necessary to do this work."

Katie also meditates regularly and has returned to Alcoholics Anonymous for regular spiritual community and to hear the spiritual principles she needs "to stay in right relationship to work, to others, and to God." She reports excellent physical and mental health as a result of these factors.

Hospice care also inspires Rita, who remains in her marriage to Tom, her bisexual husband. She has just graduated with a master's degree from a graduate school of theology and plans to be a hospice chaplain. She was led to this career goal partly through her experience of caring for a gay friend who died with AIDS. She has, in fact, found her greatest support group not in the church, but within the gay community. She has served National Affirmation and other gay activist groups and was instrumental in starting a local chapter of PFLAG. In a presentation at a Denver PFLAG meeting, Rita said, "My life has been richly blessed by my deep friendship from within the gay, lesbian, and bisexual communities, and I look forward to continuing to be a strong ally to work for total acceptance of queer people within the church and in society as a whole."

Rituals help some women promote their own wholeness. Since I stayed in our old home after Jim and I separated, I felt the need somehow to make it different—to let go of the past and its associations and to begin anew. With my meditation instructor's guidance, we planned a Lhasang, a traditional Tibetan purification ceremony. I invited my closest friends to share the experience. We chanted together the ancient words and cleansed the whole house and yard with juniper smoke. It was a symbol for me of stepping out of the past and into a new life, aspiring to be friendly to myself and merciful to others, to live mindfully and modestly and courageously. It was a way to demonstrate that I trust myself and am confident in my own Basic Goodness and that of all other sentient beings. It was a real celebration for everyone present!

Another Tibetan tradition that I found meaningful was a New Year's practice. The night before the New Year, I bathed myself as a symbolic gesture of washing away the past. Then I burned in the fireplace symbols of negative thoughts, letting go of the old emotional baggage that no longer served my new life. The idea was to step into the new year with only the *wisdom* gained from bad experiences, dedicating myself to positive thought and action.

An action doesn't have to be formalized or taught by any religious or cultural group to deepen spiritual strength. Any constructive activity that satisfies our longing for connection is useful. Gardening was a salvation for me and continues to be one of the most spiritual activities I enjoy. Touching the earth demonstrates one's place in the whole cycle of life and puts minor events into perspective. For me, working in the garden affirms the goodness of the universe. During my transition out of my marriage to Jim, gardening showed up constantly in my journal. "After digging out the huge dandelions among the raspberries, I spent some time just surveying the whole place. The garden looks lush! The clematis climbing up the porch support reaches all the way to the second floor deck and is in magnificent bloom. Its deep purple flowers are like rich, dark stars that contrast beautifully with the carpet of golden yellow moneywort covering the ground around the patio. In fact, all the summer flowers are at their best now—roses, daylilies, lavender, even early Shasta daisies. Orange and gold calendula, up from last year's seed, glow against the quiet colors of the lavender bed nearby. By next week, I can even begin picking ripe raspberries.

"Gardening here at home has inspired new appreciation for our sacred world. In even the tiniest, unnoticed things, there is *life.* Soil teems with microscopic organisms, each traveling its own path in the universe, all co-existent, all mutually dependent, all synergistic. Even when I feel confused or depressed, I'm part of that connection. I share life with even the smallest of creatures. We're all one.

"Treehouse, my home, is a feast for my eyes and heart. In every season in my garden, I work in the beds and say, "This is my favorite time of the year." It is such a privilege to touch the earth. It steadies my nerves and calms my questioning mind. I have rested deeply in this quiet, unhurried, thankful day. Now, at 9:00, I'm tired but so grateful for this sanctuary I call home."

From the time Jim came out to me until now, working with plants has fed my spirit in a unique, necessary way. I am convinced that joining nature in this way can heal emotional wounds. Creating gentle spaces of beauty is an avocation to be humbly pursued. At least it has worked for me! "Perhaps I was led to Treehouse to prepare for this vision. This home place is truly the ideal of a healing garden for me. Here, I experience nature spiritually. I'm one with the meadowlark's liquid notes, with the doe grazing unafraid only four feet away on the hill, with the raccoons that raid my vegetable patch. When I breathe out in meditation, my wall of flesh disappears and my spirit recognizes its connection with the whole. When I garden, I practice the presence of the Universal Spirit of Life. It is as Joanna Macy wrote: 'As we work to heal the Earth, the Earth heals us.'"

These examples point to just a few of the possibilities for self-healing. Exploring spiritual depths, in whatever way is natural to you, opens the possibility for freedom from anger and despair. The point is to discover some method of resting in the still center, putting wounds into a larger perspective, letting go of the past, and moving forward. To be whole and well, finding your unique version of a "healing garden" is the most worthwhile activity imaginable. In this constructive activity lie the seeds of a meaningful recovery.

7

The Result
Is the Path

A basic Buddhist concept is that every experience is a teacher: "The result is the path." My experience with my mixed orientation marriage was easily the most definitive period of my life, and the most instructive. Living it and writing about it, I see clearly that I learned necessary lessons that could only have come to me in this way. The Sanskrit word, *kshanti*, may encompass the foremost lesson. It means patience, forbearance, and calm endurance of adversity, engaging clarity, energy, and understanding. It is said that circumstances don't make the woman; they reveal her.

Their unusual circumstances removed the veils from the souls of all the women in this book and allowed them to see who they really are. Those who completed the course were eventually grateful for the lessons they learned, though they agree that the teachers in this school are very demanding.

Stages of Coping

As the previous chapters have shown, the women you've met here progressed through a number of identifiable steps, most of them moving eventually to acceptance and resolution. Similar to the process of grief, the stages of coping are summarized in *Opening the Straight Spouse's Closet*, a book published by PFLAG and based on testimony of more than two thousand straight spouses in the United States, Canada, England, and Australia. Usually, shock, relief, and confusion are followed by denial, self-blame, and sympathy. At some point, the women face reality and realize that their husbands will never be conventional spouses again. This stage is followed by anger, grief, and despair. If they have the inner strength and find some meaning beyond themselves, the women eventually begin to heal their wounds and restore their trust and hope. Finally, resolution may be achieved when anger is put aside and forgiveness is possible. Only then can a new life be built, based on the wisdom gained from experience.

It is simplistic to assume that all straight spouses travel through each of these stages in order or at the same pace. The pieces get mixed up in this very human drama, but it is clear that there is an identifiable progression, allowing for individual differences, and that all the steps emerge and sometimes repeat in some other form. Sarah, for example, said that her recovery couldn't have been speeded up. "It was a grieving process much like after a death. I know I went through all the stages within a very personal time frame." If a woman doesn't get stuck in one of the negative stages, the good news is that there is eventually an end to this process, and the outcome can actually be positive. Freedom, spiritual path, new vocation, renewed sexuality, deeper self respect—all are possible rewards. Sarah summarized her personal discoveries in this way: "I have great inner strength and I am a survivor. I believe the saying, "It's not *what* happens to you, it's *how* you react that matters." The most successful straight spouses moved to a new plateau of strength, self-awareness, and productivity, relishing the results of their hard-won degree in their unique school. Their diploma reads, "I am a whole and valuable person, with or without a partner."

Examples of Success

What are the signs that this resolution is near? Acceptance is the turning point. The man she married is still the same man now—only she knows one more important fact about him: he's gay. Whether she stays in the marriage or not, acceptance of his homosexuality is essential. It is even better if she is able maintain her love and respect for him as a valuable human being. It is also important that she recognize what may change in their situation and what is unchangeable. She *lives* the familiar serenity prayer: "God grant me the serenity to accept things I cannot change, courage to change things I can, and wisdom to know the difference." When acceptance is achieved, other healing possibilities open. Hope and trust can be restored and healthy progress begins. She makes peace with the world by making peace first with herself. This whole process may take years. It is never easy and the pace is never predictable, but it can happen.

Bonnie, for example, has adjusted to her new life amazingly well. "It was like we were closing one chapter in our lives as a family and starting a new one as a different kind of family." On her own for several years now, she is teaching at a community college and completing her master's degree in human development. The subject of her master's thesis is mixed orientation marriages, using her own experience as an example. She and her former husband are still good friends, though they live in different states. She sees no reason to cut herself off entirely from the past. "Just because I closed one chapter of my life doesn't mean I want to forget all the chapters that came before. I am grateful for the life my husband gave me. He helped me become who I am today." This statement defines this final stage of coping.

We have seen many other good examples of women who manifest healthy resolution. Rita is launching a new career in hospice work with AIDS patients, still committed to her marriage with her bisexual husband. Katie is also committed to comfort the dying, staying with them during their final days and hours. Susan and Sarah have both remarried and consciously put the pain of the past behind them. Lydia, like Bonnie, has found solace in church work. Chris is enjoying a rewarding new job as a pediatric nurse, after renewing her professional credentials and re-entering the workforce. Carlotta is happily using her advanced degrees as a professor at an urban campus of a state university. All of these women illustrate the rewards of recovery. They learned their lessons, took their exams, and passed with high marks. How they accomplished their fresh start is worth emulating.

A story from the philosopher Victor Frankl gives a clue about their winning attitudes and actions. "We who lived in the concentration camps can remember those who walked through the huts, comforting others, giving away their last piece of bread, giving proof that everything can be taken from us, but one thing, the last of human freedoms: to choose our attitude, our spirit, in any given set of circumstances."

Such abundance of spirit, the willingness to open to life as it is, characterizes the most successful women I contacted. They chose to see the good, charitable parts of their situation. The *Dhammapada*, the sayings of the Buddha, begins with the words, "Mind is the forerunner of all things." Another translation is even more direct: "We are what we think. All that we are arises with our thoughts. With our thoughts we make the world." In their mixed orientation marriages, the reality didn't change, but the wives' perception of it altered drastically. With determination to make the best of their lot, these women looked for the light, for the lesson, for the positive possibilities. They were the "straight-A students."

Manifestations of Wholeness

The women cited as examples of successful resolution had several practices in common. These noticeable traits are instructive for anyone who is on a similar journey.

1. Say what you need clearly and without apology.

In my journal, just before Jim and I separated, I was able to articulate my deep needs at the time.

"I need physical closeness."

"I need frequent reassurance of love."

"I need to touch."

"I need absolute honesty—no games, no lies."

"I need emotional support."

"I need comfortable, warm companionship."

"I need someone who enjoys doing things with me—gardening, traveling, sitting quietly to read or listen to good music."

"I need commitment."

"I need fidelity (or at least ongoing honest communication of infidelity)."

"I need to be free of the fear of AIDS."

As it turned out, Jim could not meet these needs, but my writing them down and thinking them through and discussing them with him helped us both determine our eventual course of action. It was an important step for me.

2. Live in the present.

These women live in the moment. They "rest in the 'suchness' of life," generally not dwelling on the past or worrying about the future. When I was doing meditation practice in the Shambhala Training weekends, I learned two concepts that saw me through my hardest months. First, there was a quotation by Suzuki Roshi. "Not always so," said the wise teacher. The idea that pain would eventually pass gave me hope. I was also comforted by a hand-lettered quotation on the wall of the little kitchen at the Shambhala Center. Attributed to Abraham Joshua Heschel, it read, "Just to be is a blessing. Just to live is holy." It emphasized for me that all the resources we need to live fully are already within us, if we can wake up to our own Basic Goodness and simply "be here now." The past and future are only a thought. Only the present moment and what we do in it are real. These concepts helped me to survive intact.

3. Recognize That Closure Is Important.

Recognition of the importance of closure on the pain of the past is another trait of women who reached healthy resolution. This doesn't mean that memory is erased. Rather, it implies a sense of completion, like Bonnie's analogy of closed chapters. I tried to explain my own need for closure in a letter to Jim's sister, four years after my divorce was final.

"Journey is the central issue for us both. You have yours; I have mine. In 1991, when Jim told me that he is homosexual, my world turned upside down. Everything we had worked for during our thirty-plus years of marriage changed. This was not what I planned. When it was apparent in 1995 that we couldn't make our marriage work (what was in it for me?), I had two choices, either to keep replaying the story line of loss and spend the rest of my life in bitterness, or to start all over. For the past four years, I've been working hard to recreate my life.

"I consciously let go of all the associations and baggage of my marriage, trying to heal my own wounds. Methodically, I've built a whole new self-image and through new activities have salvaged my self-esteem. My method of renewal had several fronts: writing a book about mixed orientation marriages; occasional teaching at Naropa; many hours of volunteer projects; tons of outdoor work and play, like canoeing and gardening; becoming a certified Watsu practitioner and working part-time at that; traveling; managing my investments; and just maintaining my home. The schedule is full. I joined a women's group that meets monthly and let go of the old social obligations that Jim and I did together. Last week, I learned to play poker! In fact, I took wise advice from my mother, who developed all new activities and interests after Daddy's death, because it was too painful for her to do alone what they had done together.

"I've also made a spiritual commitment to a philosophy that emphasizes staying in the present and letting go of aggression and neurosis. My marriage and career in business with Jim were my entire identity. I lost both, but my Buddhist training came at exactly the time I had to have it: 'When the student is ready, the teacher appears.' Now I'm starting over with Dale, a friend of fifteen years. He has also helped me to regain perspective. All these factors are helping me bring closure to the past so that I can move forward in a healthy way."

Making conscious changes in many small activities and interests, it is possible to create a whole new perspective. At the same time, it is important to remember whatever is good about the past. When the selective memory effort is successful, it demonstrates a concept from *A Course in Miracles:* "All your past except its beauty is gone, and nothing is left but a blessing."

4. See Yourself as Complete.

A fourth manifestation of resolution among the women in the book is that they see themselves as complete—single or married, with or without a partner. During all the years that Jim and I were married, I always used the pronoun, we. "We want to do this or that." After our separation, I had to teach myself to say "I," speaking just for myself.

Carlotta experienced the same thing. Now she says, "I love where I am. My former husband and his partner are an important part of my life, but I'm on my own. My children are taking wing, and I am now thinking about the next five years."

Sandy also feels satisfied with her life as a single parent, though she is open to having another romantic relationship. The point is that she knows she can be happy either way. "I carry my happiness with me. I'm not looking for anyone to make me whole or full or complete. I'm working on doing that myself and I feel pretty good about myself. I don't put up with anything in a relationship that takes away from my dignity, but I also feel that I'm strong enough and healthy enough to give responsibly in a relationship, too.... I don't see that I'm less than whole by not being part of a couple. I think being part of a couple is just a bonus."

Becoming strong enough to stand alone may be one of the unexpected benefits of experiencing, then leaving a mixed orientation marriage.

5. You Are Not a Victim.

This leads to another manifestation of resolution. The women who emerged intact do not consider themselves victims. There is not a trace of self-pity in their conversation. They don't blame their husbands. Sarah, for example, feels no bitterness now, "Even knowing what I have gone through—indescribable pain, like a long, drawn-out surgery without anesthetic. Although there was a time I wished Tim had died—I thought that would have been easier."

Looking back from the perspective she has now, Sarah feels very differently. After sharing her story with me, she said, "Each time I go through this, it's an affirmation of the good that can come from a painful experience. "We have a son who has grown up to be a wonderful, talented, gentle-hearted man, husband, and artist. Tim and I have healed our pain by letting go of what could not be, yet holding on to what has always been between us—a love deep in our souls for each other."

Today, Sarah is at peace as a physically and emotionally healthy woman. "I am married to a man who has helped me to grow intellectually and to strengthen my physical condition by taking up running, backpacking, and biking. He has helped me to discover my sexuality and take delight in it, and is not threatened by the parts of me that still belong to the other two men in my life, my son and Tim."

Similarly, Carlotta is in a calm place with Daniel and herself. "Our focus is on the family unit that still exists, because we have children that we both love very much." Yet, Carlotta is successfully recreating her separate life. "I've become again the person I was before I got married—and it feels good. I have transitioned to another place. Things are different and I want to enjoy the difference. Knowing I can do things, like build a house, do our own divorce, and remain friends, is significant to me. I'm amazed at how happy I am. I feel that I have grown through my independence."

Sarah and Carlotta are evidence of Ralph Waldo Emerson's assertion that "The measure of mental health is the disposition to find good everywhere." I concur. Rereading my own journal, I also experience again the fear, revelation, torment, joy, anger, cosmic questions, and recent peace that have changed my life. I never dreamed there could be such dramatic evolution, such incredible contrast of feelings. During the years since 1991, I lost, then found faith and spirituality, my personal identity, and my relationship with Jim. As the writer, Albert Camus, said, "What doesn't kill me, makes me stronger." Paradoxically, however, through two deaths, my father's and my marriage, I better understand life. While my evolution will never end, I have at least reached deeper understanding. My life is better now. I am healthier now. Far from being a victim, I am grateful for the journey.

Lessons Learned

This entire book is made up of lessons learned, but it may be useful to summarize the most important ones. Each reader may draw her own priority list of insights, but here are my conclusions.

- Living a lie is hell. Authenticity is the highest aspiration.

- There are no accidents. We somehow choose the events of our lives in order to learn what our spirits need. Everything is a teacher for those who are awake.

- People may not love you the way you'd choose, but that doesn't mean they don't love you with all they have.

- "No one is ever, always fortunate." (Euripides, in *The Trojan Women*)

- We have the right to be angry sometimes, but that doesn't give us the right to be cruel.

- Accepting what is makes it possible to let go of what can't change.

- The greatest power is to create change in your own life.

- Perception is reality and we move toward our dominant thought. By intentionally changing negative thought patterns, we can heal emotional wounds.

- Our deepest delusion is the sense of ourselves as separate. All spirit is one and we are intrinsically connected to all beings. Therefore, we can have compassion. Therefore, we are never alone.

- Finally, I know that I have everything I need to live the life I choose.

That day in the garden when Jim cried with me over his confession of homosexuality seems so distant now, another lifetime. This book was begun four different times in the pain of self-therapy, but it has ended in the joy of love. Love, finally, is the fabric of true transformation. And its possibilities are endless. "Only that day dawns to which we are awake," Thoreau said in *Walden*. "There is more day to dawn. The sun is but a morning star." Good morning! I have no regrets.

8

Epilogue
Their Journey Continues

We have met many courageous women in the pages of this book. Their stories create a broad picture of meaningful struggle and in many cases triumph. Viewed as a whole, their experiences illustrate the possibility of recovery and personal progress. But where are these women now? What has happened to them since they candidly talked with me? As their journey continues inside or beyond the closet, how do they feel? After writing the book, I asked them for an update.

Alice maintains a cheerful outlook, despite her recent diagnosis of multiple sclerosis. She says, "I feel normal," and she sounds optimistic. She has only occasional attacks of the MS and says that it is not progressive. She is dealing with her manic-depression with medication and is "more even-keeled than before." The best news is that she is happily remarried and feels that her children are also doing well now. She is thrilled about the prospect of welcoming her first grandchild. "It's good that they can see that everyone can get along."

Alice enjoys working as a receptionist in a dental office, a post she's held for nearly three years. With some distance and healing time since her divorce, she can now say, "I have a wonderful ex-husband and a wonderful husband. The way it turned out is good for all of us."

Andrea, now in her early fifties, is enjoying a good relationship and spends time in volunteer work, housekeeping, gardening, and spiritual practice." While she still experiences depression and some anger, "it is on the back burner and not particularly bother-some." Though no longer in contact with her former husband, she expresses compassion for him and his new mate: "It helps to remember how much pain he must have been in, struggling to appear straight and having a secret gay life. He has remarried, though, so I assume he is still living that way and is still in the closet. Maybe I'm wrong. I hope so. It makes me sad and mad to know another woman is probably experiencing what I experienced."

Andrea says that her most valuable lesson from all this is "that honesty and integrity are essential for a healthy relationship." She vows, "Never again to tolerate such silence, deception, and great emotional pain."

Annie has learned after eight years that she can survive and be happy as a single person. "I'm quite able to entertain myself and get what I need." She spends part of her time in classes, enjoys good friends, and is feeling independent. "I trust myself and I'm not desperate for a relationship." Though she feels both her sons were damaged psychologically by the anger and confusion during her marriage to their gay father, she says that they are also better now.

Annie's advice is to "get as healthy as you can, whatever that takes." She is still in therapy. Learning to like herself better helped her most. Having gained more confidence, she is able to "pull on internal resources now." She feels "consistent, reliable, and loving" toward her sons. For Annie, pain was her motivator to improve her life from the inside out.

Beth is happy, healthy, and recovered, noting that her breakup with Bart, her gay lover, happened twenty years ago, "and it took some time, maybe five years in all, to get over it. I did remain friends with Bart until his death last year. I still feel sad at times about his death and sometimes dream about him. Occasionally, I'm angry with him for contracting AIDS and dying prematurely. Yet I also feel enriched by our friendship. So the whole experience has been very mixed and very complex. After all, it was a thirty-three-year-long relationship, if you include the friendship before and after the five years we were a couple. Like my other oldest friends, I felt that there were many threads to our relationship and that often we had a kind of understanding that could turn on a word or phrase that had behind it the depth of many years and many experiences together. We could appreciate who we were and who we had been. At his memorial service, his family asked me to speak as his best friend."

In the past two decades, Beth has built a satisfying life as a psychologist, busy with family, friends, clients, writing, traveling, and teaching. Her life is full and her relationship with her husband is "very happy," with "none of the feelings of physical rejection" she formerly felt with her gay partner. "My husband and I have a great deal of love, understanding, and humor between us, with none of the dark clouds of that earlier love." Still, she says she wouldn't change the enriching experience she had with Bart. Over the years her family and even her husband became good friends with him, "so I think some of this was healing and that he finally became like family in a different way than I had earlier wanted."

Beth's most important lesson was to recognize relationships for what they can be and are, not what you wish they could be. She recognizes the impossibility of changing a person's sexual orientation—no matter how much you wish that could happen. She believes that her experience with a gay lover taught her a great deal about her "intra-psychic dynamics" and eventually made her a better therapist.

Betty has "grown into a strong survivor as a straight spouse." Despite her constantly declining physical health, her mental health status is "great." She notes that her thirty-year career as a nurse ended in March 1998, when she became unable to work because of the severity of her own illness. She struggled through the Social Security system and finally began receiving disability payments in the spring of 1999. This financial help gives her a bit more security. Her children are faring much better now, as well. "They have dealt with adult topics and survived," she says.

With time and distance, Betty has also achieved more clarity about her husband's character. "My ex-husband's lack of responsibility regarding child support has nothing to do with his gay lifestyle." She no longer blames his homosexuality for his hurtful actions toward her and the children. She has concluded that his sexual orientation is innate; his violent and deceptive actions were choices.

Bonnie has restored her balance and happiness remarkably well. Having lived a thousand miles from her ex-husband for more than five years, she says, "My past as a straight spouse doesn't often cross my mind." Still, she feels gratitude for the twenty-nine years of her marriage. "Sometimes, I think the pain would have been less, had we not shared such a strong, close relationship in our marriage; but we were able to have in our time together what some persons never attain in fifty or sixty years." Though Bonnie would have preferred to remain happily married to "the wonderful man who was my husband," she knew it had to end "when he met his soul mate and could no longer honor our vows and remain as the husband I had known."

Bonnie has carried out her determination to change her life in positive ways. "Through faith and attitude, I have chosen to be content and happy" by moving on. She has spent the past five years building her new life. She is a sorority housemother, teaches classes at the local community college and is concluding her master's program in human development. In the meantime she has remained very active in her church, serving on the cabinet and as a department chair. Her physical health is the best ever since she began working out regularly with a mini-trampoline and weightlifting. She says the exercise is "incredibly invigorating. Mentally, I feel better than I ever have."

Bonnie's three sons and their families remain very close to her and also to Stan. "Extended family and friends from church still care a lot about both my ex and me." She describes her present relationship with Stan as platonic. They stay in touch as necessary on family matters, but she no longer feels any emotional ties. She recently entered a promising new relationship "with a man who has the same values and interests in life." Though there were "lots of lonely years in between, I do know that I can once again trust a man and in that I rejoice!"

Bonnie's clearest insight from her experience is the value of her faith. She learned that "life can shatter at a moment's notice." But through her religious conviction, she was able to pick up the pieces. She also expresses the hope that the telling of her story and that of other women will be a positive influence on other mixed orientation couples. "If we can help even one family not go through what we did, then re-living all of these memories will not have been done in vain."

Carlotta has also emerged whole and healthy, half a decade after her divorce. "I don't see the experience as a negative, but rather what is." She always refers to him as her former husband, not her ex, explaining that their separation is respectful and that she wants others to treat it that way. She considers Daniel and his male partner a couple, who are her very dear friends. "I know I can rely on them and that they are there for me." For Carlotta, the disclosure of Daniel's sexual orientation was less painful than their divorce—which they both agreed was the right course of action.

But she is moving past that pain as well. She feels proud of her independence. Since the time Daniel came out, Carlotta has had major surgery, moved into a new house, taken a new job, and adjusted to having both her children leave the nest. In the meantime, she ran for city council—twice! "I have to remember what I can do—what I am good at and what problems I can solve. My values haven't changed. If I want to feel pity for myself, it doesn't have to be about Daniel."

If she ever enters another romantic relationship, Carlotta will look for several differences. She wants closer companionship, mutual independence, and more spontaneity. "I don't want to lose myself," she summarizes. Even though it requires hard work, Carlotta is determined to create her own life in her own way. She's dreaming about a good future and concludes: "The world as I know it depends on what I make of it. And I can make it one wonderful place for me."

Carol. I am also feeling fulfilled and healed, five years after my divorce. Like every other ex-wife, I had many mixed emotions, but writing it down helped immensely to sort them out. It seems clear now that I was in deep denial about how hurt I really was, even fooling myself. Looking back, I was more dysfunctional than I realized, and Jim and I remained co-dependent for a long time after we separated. Jim's move to California was good for us both, and now we are both healthier and happier. We see each other occasionally and our relationship is warm and friendly. It is important to us both to keep that balance, because we value our history and our ties with our children and other family members.

Happily, I have enjoyed a loving relationship with a long-time friend, which has grown deeper over the past four years. Like Carlotta, I had a very difficult time ending my first marriage and was resistant to making that commitment again. "Till death do us part" was a vow I took seriously and literally. But I've come to understand that the Jim who was my husband did "die" and has been reincarnated in a whole new life. I stayed with him through his death as a straight man and his birth as a gay one. I have a new life as well, recently remarrying. I'm free to promise to love my new husband "as long as we both shall live." I feel extremely fortunate to find happiness beyond the closet in a worthwhile new life. Repeating the ending of the final chapter: "I have no regrets."

Cherie continues her work with childcare and is still very happy as a straight spouse. She feels "enriched and fortunate to have a bisexual husband," as her marriage with Roy remains satisfying for them both. She says, "My relationship with my husband is close, sweet, amazing, and the greatest gift God has given me." Cherie is a model for a heterosexual woman who knowingly chooses to marry a gay or bisexual man. She says, "The most valuable lesson I have learned is that one can never be sure of the package one's soul mate may arrive in."

Chris is again enjoying her nursing profession in a pediatric office. She feels that her self-esteem is the best ever and has been able to maintain friendly contact with her estranged husband. He is still actively involved in the lives of their three children and supports them financially. "They know he's a good father," Chris says. Regarding her recovery after this experience, Chris advises other women to give it time. She is thankful for the twenty good years their family shared and is now strong enough to work toward a satisfying, independent future.

Katie is glad to report excellent physical and mental health. She attributes her good condition to meditation, a recent therapy session with her ex-husband, and resumption of regular attendance at Alcoholics Anonymous. Still working through her gay/straight issues more than twenty years after her divorce, she quotes the A.A. teaching: "Do not regret the past, nor wish to shut the door on it."

Katie and her former husband have occasional conversations and meetings through their three grown children. She actually feels grateful that she will be forced to grow continually as long as she is in contact with him. Just last year, she realized that they both had habitually engaged in manipulative behaviors aimed at staying connected—even though it was draining both of them. They had one therapy session together that allowed them to "see the hooks." The result was a mutual commitment to "let go and stop engaging in those behaviors."

Katie summarized what she has learned. "I needed circumstances to be this dramatic so that I would have an inescapable reason to let go and could thus see what my own true problems were. I had no self-esteem and desperately needed to be loved. And I was so dependent on my ex-husband and so enmeshed with him through my manipulative behavior that I would never have let go had he been straight. As a result, I most likely would never have looked at my behavior, let alone changed it and thus my life. So for this soul, this was the perfect relationship."

Katie also values the reflection required to contribute to this book. "I feel that I have gained a sense of peace and acceptance that had been eluding me. It's good to tell the story and especially good to know that it might in some way benefit others."

Joni says that her life now is "much better professionally and personally." A year after her divorce, she is in a healthy relationship and feels very fortunate that she "fell in love with the right man this time around." She thrives on her work as a special education teacher and stays fit by running, skiing, and dancing. She regularly writes in her journals and enjoys reading during her quiet times.

While Joni feels happy and whole again, she is saddened by David's refusal to be friends with her. She says, "I do still miss him. I want him to be happy." They are in touch only for necessary business questions, such as the sale of a jointly owned piece of property. Joni is hurt that David rejects any friendly contact. "I want us to be able to go down to the coffeehouse and share our lives. Unfortunately, David is not ready to do that, especially since his partner is insecure about me." David doesn't want to be reminded of the pain that they both went through, so Joni is "trying to learn to accept not seeing him again or being friends."

Through it all, Joni has maintained her optimism and looks forward to a bright future. She says that her gay/straight experience helped her discover her own strength and made her more understanding with others.

Kaye and Joseph are still married and seem to have evolved into ever-deeper understanding and acceptance. Joseph is till her best friend. "He is more grounded than he ever has been before—more responsive and invested" in their relationship. As Kaye plans her retirement from her work with infants and young families, she is enjoying relatively good health, though managing rheumatoid arthritis. She says she is content, but more reserved than she used to be. She continues in therapy, hoping to resolve issues from her childhood that might have played a part in her choosing a gay mate.

Kaye's main difficulty at present is a lingering distance from their daughter, who is still hurt by the "necessary lies" during all the years before Joseph came out to the family. The young woman hasn't completely withdrawn, but "does have a firmer boundary drawn between us." Kaye misses the "old easy friendship" with her.

Still, after nearly forty years of marriage, Kaye is glad that she made the decision to stay with Joseph. "Loving him goes far beyond his strengths or faults. It shifts onto a new plane of awareness and experience every time we come to an impasse. With each one, there is a time of awful turmoil and hurt or anger—then a calming—and a new landscape."

And each time that new landscape appears, she says, all the old ones remain as backdrop to the new. Clearly, these two people love each other enough to endure the painful times in order to enjoy each new vista.

Laura is also still in her marriage and spends her free time as she always has, volunteering at church. She and her husband "are both doing fine. We both feel that at this stage of life (ages 79 and 77), neither one of us wants a new relationship. Besides, we still love each other. My husband did not choose to be gay, any more than I chose to be heterosexual."

Still, she says that forgiveness is the major lesson learned through her mixed orientation marriage. She's optimistic, however. She and her husband are busy preparing for a major life change, sorting through thirty-eight years worth of accumulated possessions in order to sell their home and move to new quarters. Once settled, they look forward to taking computer classes together, "so we can become proficient enough to get on the Internet and tap into National Geographic, national libraries, etc." Laura has fully accepted her situation and is content and happy. She summarizes, "We are living our lives to the fullest."

Lee has a demanding and rewarding twelve-year career as a systems analyst at a large government installation. She is putting all her energy into her future, rather than dwelling on the painful past, though she and Randy are still in touch and occasionally have dinner or go camping together. Her main regret is that she chose to "live in limbo" for so many years, unable to take any decisive action toward her own fulfillment. "I lived my life as a big lie for a very long time. A lie that I never in my wildest dreams had even thought of. I was shoved in the closet with him, not by my own choosing. Currently, the most important thing to me is honesty."

One important piece of advice Lee offers is to decide exactly what your own goals are. When she and Randy decided to divorce, she thought through her most important values and focused her attention on them. "I wanted my daughter, my dog, and my retirement benefits. I wanted to be living in my own house, the house that *I* chose." Lee kept sight of these specific goals and largely disregarded anything that would interfere with them. Though she is not living the life she envisioned as an innocent bride twelve years ago, Lee is now an independent, confident woman with a bright future.

Lydia wryly summarizes her experience in this way: "The married years were fine and now is fine. The middle years between were difficult." She feels relieved that Jonathan came out and now the transition is over. The tension was gone when he was gone from the household." Today, she is happy in her work and her community. "I am free to do what I want, when I want. I am most grateful every day." Her profession in social work helps elder people remain independent, as well. And her volunteer work with the Alliance on Aging, the YWCA, her church, and the Inter-racial Women's Club reinforces her sense of accomplishment.

After years of tumult, Lydia's three children are "wonderful—very caring, grateful, and attentive." Now in her fifties, she is in relative good health with high blood pressure under control through medication. "I am comfortable, not fearful or upset," she says. She has begun to recognize that her husband's "selfish, private style was probably a result of his need to get out of the marriage—and he did not know how to do it."

Lydia added an interesting sidelight to her history. While she feels now that she probably should have let go of the marriage two or three years before her husband moved out, she was clinging to "that comfort zone—having money to support the family." Her self-image enters in: "I guess I had a concept that whatever work I did or whatever money I generated was for the extra things—the summer trips, the car, the savings account. I was an accessory! I had an education, but I chose to be a stay-at-home mother. We had three children, all born within eighteen months. I was older and stayed home to assist in the children's activities and be a supportive parent. I still believe that is a very important role."

It seems that Lydia has reconciled all this and feels empowered in her new independence. "I believe that I was and am capable of doing whatever I choose to do." The process of talking about this history has also been helpful to her. She said it was "very interesting and a great exercise in bringing back some of the events of my life. I am grateful for this opportunity." Like the other women in this book, she wants to help anyone in a mixed orientation marriage survive intact.

Maya loves her work as Director of Cultural Programs at a busy urban library. Long remarried, she has had nearly twenty years to process her experience as a straight spouse and to move on with her life. Her three children have presented her with six grandchildren. Her health is good and she is settled and satisfied.

Rita completed her master of divinity degree in May, 1999, and is realizing her dream of working as a chaplain with the local hospice. She works in a large metropolitan area and visits patients in hospitals and nursing homes all over the city. She is relieved to be through with her academic program and elated to be doing her chosen life work. Her husband continues in his computer work, and their relationship remains close.

Rita reiterated her best advice for others in mixed orientation marriages: "Don't panic and keep communicating." Her ability to be happy in her own marriage demonstrates the power of her message.

Sandy has learned a great deal about herself and her own patterns through her gay/straight marriage. She believes that her exhusband chose her because she was strong and he felt safe with her. But she also had her own reasons for "hiding out in the relationship." By leaving the marriage, she faced her demons and took responsibility for her own life. Though the introspective process was painful, "I am stronger and more comfortable with who I am, having worked through the struggles."

Sandy's work as a fiction buyer for a growing library system is satisfying and challenging. She says the job makes her feel comfortable and competent; she is proud of her contributions to the organization. She is very close to her eight-year-old daughter, who has also become calmer during the past year. "There was much good, along with the bad of my marriage, and my daughter is by far the best of those years."

A change that resulted from her whole experience is to take care of issues as they arise, rather than waiting until a problem is out of proportion. This insight applies to interpersonal relationships and to her own health care. She no longer simply endures and suffers through pain. Rather, she pays conscious attention to her mental and physical health, because she knows she's worth the effort.

Sandy recognizes some important lessons. First, face the fact of your husband's homosexuality directly. "If I had faced James' grappling with his sexuality earlier in our marriage, instead of hoping the issues would go away, we might have been able to remain friends." This implies seeking information about homosexuality and bisexuality. Use the library and the Internet, she advises. "Information truly is power, especially in times when one feels alone, facing an uncertain future."

A second major lesson is to support, trust, and respect your own integrity. Be available to others, but walk away if asked to diminish or give up your own needs to please another. She quotes Alexandra Stoddard's book, *Making Choices: The Joy of a Courageous Life:*

"Actively say no. When you say good-bye to the weeds you didn't plant, you make room for the flowers of your choice."

Finally, Sandy believes that she has one last hurdle before she can completely put her old marriage behind her. "I must learn to forgive James for not being strong enough to be who he really was sooner." This forgiveness is her "final undertaking in moving on, in putting that chapter of my life to rest."

Sarah shines as an example of resilience. Self-described as a "chronically happy person, from birth to fifty-four years of age," she feels healthy and secure with friends and family who have loved and supported her through all her life's transitions. Though her union with a gay man provided both high and low points, she feels "recovered from the depression and chaos of the breakup of the marriage." But she never wants to turn her back on "the love invested in that person." She and her ex-husband are still very close. They talk often, correspond, and visit. She says, "We spend about a week together each summer, enjoying the relationship we've built over thirty-seven years, since we met in college." She adds, "These visits are with my present husband's blessings."

The concept of family is very broad in Sarah's case. It includes her ex-husband and his family, their son and his wife, and her present husband and his family. She has been happily married to this second husband for eleven years and they are looking forward to an active retirement next year when she concludes her career as an elementary school teacher.

Sarah offers others the wisdom she has gleaned from all this. "It's not what happens to us in our lives, it's how we deal with events that makes the experience enrich or ruin our lives." The idea of choice recurs in her thoughts. "I chose to share my life with a caring, moral, motivated, funny, and lovable man. We chose to have and raise a son together. We chose to go toward separate futures when staying together would cause pain. The pain is gone; the love remains. How fortunate we are!"

Susan remembers that her experience as a straight spouse was "very disturbing and all-consuming at the time," but she now feels happy and fulfilled in her second marriage. She enjoys many common interests with her new husband, spending time traveling and honing their tennis and golf games. Susan feels fortunate that her children "seem to have accepted their father for who he is," though they still feel some tension with him. Their daughter lives only four doors away from Susan, so she sees her ex-husband frequently when he visits there. Their present relationship is friendly.

Susan is conservative in her view of homosexuality. She believes that "the gay society today is very strong and they are determined to make their sexual orientation acceptable." She opposes teaching about it in the schools and abhors the thought of homosexual marriages. Her way of coping with these negative thoughts has simply been to move on in her life to the things she admires and enjoys, not dwelling on the past.

Sylvia looks to her close friends as her support system. "I am doing great. I have a whole web of friends I consider family." She also visits frequently with a group of Benedictine Sisters and finds it helpful to talk openly with them. She counsels that the first year is the hardest, then it gets easier. Citing her faith, she says, "all unpleasant things happen to produce good." She and her former husband both teach at the same school and are on friendly terms.

Vera is a retired teacher who truly enjoys an active life with many close friends. Now seventy-five, she says, "I'm a happy, busy widow with a totally new life." She is enthusiastic about duplicate bridge and plays at golf. Active in her church, she has also traveled extensively. None of her friends know the full truth about her marriage. She still chooses to keep her secrets to herself.

Before her husband's death with AIDS, she also kept busy "to lessen the pain." She wrote a children's book and won two outstanding teacher awards. She recognizes the positive aspects of her experience. If her husband had not left the Air Force, she would have missed twenty-three years as a teacher. "My career was so rewarding and my income now is greater than it would have been." If she could change anything, she says it would be to "be braver than I was and just get the divorce—not believe that things would get better."

Zoe has now been married to her bisexual husband for more than nine years. She is "his best friend" and appreciates what he has taught her: to be more compassionate with herself. He helps her avoid her old patterns of self-deprecation and blame. They both enjoy their "community within the home," after adopting a Chinese daughter, now three years old. Her greatest insight from her mixed orientation marriage is that sexual orientation cannot be changed: "This isn't their fault." Her marriage meets most of her needs and, as a Buddhist, she is grateful for its "path quality."

Appendix
Additional Resources

This resource list was compiled from suggestions from the women interviewed for the book. It is not meant to be an exhaustive bibliography. Rather, it identifies materials that these straight spouses found useful. It is offered as a starting point for those who follow on this path, with the advice to keep searching until satisfying personal answers emerge for your own questions.

Organizations

Straight Spouse Network (SSN)
Amity Pierce Buxton, Director
8215 Terrace Drive
El Cerrito, CA 94530-3058
Phone: 510-525-0200
Internet: www.ssnetwk.org
info@ssnetwk.org

Children of Lesbians and Gays Everywhere (COLAGE)
3543 18th Street, #17
San Francisco, CA 94110
Phone: 415-861-5437
Internet: COLAGE@colage.org
Support and information for children of gay, lesbian, bisexual, and transgender parents. Offers a Web page, newsletter, and pen pals.

Parents, Families and Friends of Lesbians and Gays (PFLAG)
1726 M Street NW, Suite 400
Washington, DC 20036
Phone: 202-467-8180
Internet: www.pflag.org

Sex Information and Education Counsel of the United States
130 W. 42nd Street, Suite 350
New York, NY 10036
Phone: 212-819-9770

AIDS Information

National Pediatric AIDS Network, resource for information on HIV/AIDS, especially in young people. See "HIV: The Basics"
Internet: www.npan.org

Updated, general information on AIDS
Internet: www.aidscentral.com

Mothers' Voices for AIDS, an educational organization
Internet: www.mvoices.org

Books

Beattie, Melody. *Beyond Codependency*. Harper and Row, 1989. (The chapter called "Overcoming Fatal Attractions" is especially recommended.)

Bozett, Frederick W. and Sussman, M.B., eds. *Homosexuality and Family Relations*. Harrington, 1988. (Collection of articles on family relationship issues.)

Buxton, Amity Pierce. *The Other Side of the Closet: The Coming-Out Crisis for Straight Spouses and Families*. Revised edition, Wiley, 1994. (Comprehensive study of family trauma, based on research by an experienced counselor.)

Clark, Donald Henry. *The New Loving Someone Gay*. Celestial Arts, 1987. (Helpful in dispelling prejudices and confusion.)

Corley, Andre. *The Final Closet*. Editech, 1990. (Discusses appropriate ways to talk with children about homosexuality.)

Gochros, Jean Schaar. *When Husbands Come Out of the Closet*. Harrington, 1989. (Academic, thorough approach to the subject.)

Hill, Ivan. *The Bisexual Spouse*. Harper, 1987. (Ethical issues raised by bisexuality within marriage.)

Lerner, Harriet. *Life Preservers: Staying Afloat in Love and Life*. HarperCollins, 1996. (Various situations covered, including the straight spouse dilemma.)

Pearson, Carol Lynn. *Goodbye, I Love You*. Jove, 1989. (Autobiographical account by a Mormon woman whose husband comes out, leaves the marriage, then returns home to be nursed by his ex-wife through his final illness with AIDS.)

Rogak, Lisa A. *Pretzel Logic: A Novel*. Williams Hill, 1999. (Fictionalized account of the personal experience of the author as a straight spouse.)

Stoddard, Alexandra. *Making Choices: The Joy of a Courageous Life.* William Morrow and Company, 1994. (Helpful aid to wholeness, after the crisis is over.)

Whitney, Catherine. *Uncommon Lives: Gay Men and Straight Women.* New American, 1990. (Based on interviews with mixed orientation couples, both married and unmarried.)

OTHER BOOKS BY THE CROSSING PRESS

For Women Who Grieve: Embracing Life After the Death of Your Partner

By Tangea Tansley

Drawing on her experience and hard won insights following her husband's unexpected death, Tansley provides compassionate, practical help to women.

Paper • ISBN 0-89594-832-X

A Foxy Old Woman's Guide to Traveling Alone

By Jay Ben-Lesser

A delightful hoot that will appeal to travelers of all ages. Put on your sensible shoes and get ready for a reading treat! —Library Journal

Paper • ISBN 0-89594-789-7

From Wedded Wife to Lesbian Life: Stories of Transformation

Edited by Deborah Abbott and Ellen Farmer

...deals on a compelling, personal level with most of the problems facing lesbians, especially those who have been married—conflicts with family, custody battles, financial strains, struggles to achieve independence and a sense of wholeness. —Ellen Lewin, Ph.D., author of Lesbian Mothers

Paper • ISBN 0-89594-766-8

Healing Spirits: True Stories from 14 Spiritual Healers

By Judith Joslow-Rodewald and Patricia West-Barker

Photographs by Susan Mills

In an attempt to turn a fantasy into reality, three women, Judith Joslow-Rodewald, Patricia West-Barker, and Susan Mills, traveled across the United States to meet, learn from, and record the stories of practicing healers. These healers' stories and paths are both ordinary and extraordinary, but what they all share is an unshakable belief in the idea that everyone is a potential healer with an innate ability to move toward wholeness.

Paper • ISBN 1-58091-064-5

On Women Turing Forty: Coming Into Our Fullness

By Cathleen Rountree

These candid interviews and beautiful photographs will inspire all women who are navigating through the mid-life passage. The updated look of this best-selling classic makes it the perfect companion to the later decades of Rountree's series on women.

Paper • ISBN 0-89594-517-7

Resolving Conflict Sooner: The Powerfully Simple 4-Step Method for Reaching Better Agreements More Easily in Everyday Life

By Kare Anderson

Kare Anderson gives us four simple steps to *Resolving Conflict Sooner.* Through these four simple steps, Kare shows us how conflict can be an opportunity for people to come together, connect, and establish a deeper connection.

Paper • ISBN 0-89594-976-8

Sister Outsider: Essays & Speeches

By Audre Lorde

Among the elements that make the book so good are its personal honesty and lack of pretentiousness. —New York Times

Paper • ISBN 0-89594-141-4

Women's Ventures, Women's Visions: 29 Inspiring Stories from Women Who Started Their Own Businesses

By Shoshana Alexander

Alexander presents profiles of 29 remarkable women who found a way to establish their own enterprises and realize their dreams. Despite their diversity in age, socio-economic class, and ethnic background, they are not that different from all of us who have a desire for financial independence.

Paper • ISBN 0-89594-823-0

For a current catalog of books from The Crossing Press visit our Web site at:**www.tenspeed.com**